THE VIEW FROM RAPPAHANNOCK
II

THE VIEW FROM RAPPAHANNOCK
II

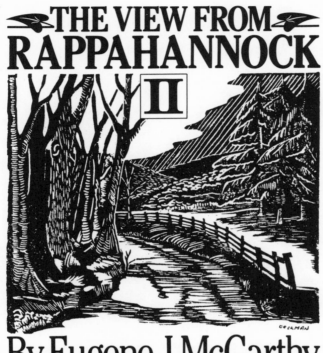

By Eugene J. McCarthy

EPM PUBLICATIONS
McLEAN, VIRGINIA

Library of Congress Cataloging in Publication Date

McCarthy, Eugene J., 1916–
   The view from Rappahannock II.

   1. Rappahannock County (Va.)—Social life and customs.
2. Rappahannock County (Va.)—Description and travel.
I. Title.   II. Title: View from Rappahannock 2.
III. Title: View from Rappahannock two.
F232.R2M34 1989   975.5′395   89-1640
ISBN 0-939009-19-6

EPM Publications, Inc., 1003 Turkey Run Road McLean, VA 22101
Printed in the United States of America

Book and cover design by Tom Huestis

Block prints by Barbara S. Bockman

CONTENTS

Fences

Rappahannock Revisited

A Second Look

RAPPAHANNOCK COUNTY has not changed very much since I wrote about it five years ago. It is still 75 miles and 75 years away from Washington, D.C. The ruins of old mills still mark the courses of small rivers, runs, and creeks. The number of churches, roughly 50, serving slightly more than 5,000 persons, or souls (one church to 100), is about what it was five years ago. A few church buildings have been given over to other than religious purposes, in a way reborn or reincarnated. Neither word quite applies. In one case, an Episcopal church in Sperryville has been deconsecrated and is now a craft shop, which would seem to be, if a church had to go, a good way to go. The number of post offices at last count is still nine, approximately one for every 500 persons, or one post office for every ten churches. There is, as was the case five years ago, no drug store and no liquor store in the county and nothing that could be called a supermarket or a shopping mall. Population growth has been minimal, close to zero, and the Gross County Product, the local equivalent of the Gross National Product, has been stable, that is, somewhat short of the reported national level. The sub- or secret-economic statistics for the county have never been firmly established. A cursory survey indicates that, as previously, most residents of the county, in the event of a nuclear war would rather see or meet Carrol Jenkins approaching with his pick-up truck, chain saw, and other equipment rather than the President of the United States in a helicopter or the Secretary of Defense in an M1 tank.

Reverend Jenks Hobson remains the most trusted clergyman of the county, as attested to by the fact that he still is asked to bless the hounds at the opening of the Fall Hunt. He has been asked why, in the course of his blessing the day before the hunt, which includes the riders, the horses, the hounds and the fox or foxes, he does not include the chickens that are scattered along the prospective route of the ride. Buster Hitt is looked upon as the person most to be trusted if you are interested in used cars, and Junior Baldwin, if you live in the western part of the county, as the best repairman, far superior to Mr. Goodwrench or the Midas man. The groundhog remains the most despised and hated animal in the county, especially by James Kilpatrick, nationally known columnist and a great nature lover, who, it is reported, remains hopeful that a scroll may be found in some high Judean cave establishing that the Biblical curse that mentions thorns and thistles also included groundhogs, thereby giving him scriptural support for his natural case against that animal.

The heavy discussions of national and international problems take place three or four times a week during the lunch period at the Corner Post Restaurant in Flint Hill. More immediate, and possibly more pressing problems are dealt with in the early morning gatherings at the W. and J. store on Route 231 beyond Sperryville, a store noted as the "last stop" (depending on what you may be stopping for) before Old Rag Mountain.

Actually, what takes place is not so much a gathering as a kind of moving or fluid discussion in which the participants come and go. In the course of the hour and a half from seven-thirty to nine o'clock, on any morning of the week, participants in the discussions may include woodcutters and wood haulers, horse and mule traders, a rattle snake hunter, a game warden, a sheriff's deputy, a photographer, orchard men, lawyers, haymakers, and others. The military is represented principally by colonels, although occasionally, in the absence of the established colonels, someone will acknowledge that he was something less than a colonel. The whole proceeding is managed by Wilma Burke who runs the store. Not all storekeepers in Rappahannock County are owned or run by Burkes, but it seems to be better, if one is in the store-keeping profession, to be a Burke or to be married to one. Consumer protection is taken care of at W. and J.'s principally by anticipation of trouble, preventive action. The banana, occasionally offered for sale, is the only fresh fruit ever available and the tomato, the only fresh vegetable. The staple offerings in the fresh or natural order are potatoes and standard onions of good size and not of any of the varieties that are advertised as not causing eyes to water, or as tasting like apples.

The store itself, at least in the morning hours, is a kind of sanctuary. Privacy is respected. Any exaggeration is tolerated and allowed, even encouraged, unless it downgrades the character of some person. There are no limits on what may be told, of war, of coon hounds, of fox hounds or of beagles, of game sightings, and success in hunting. I have reported having seen as many as thirty wild turkeys in a flock, three bears, and three bob-cats without noting any raised eyebrows. Reports on mountain lions are more suspect, only one sighting claimed by John Glasker having gone unchallenged. Reports of success in betting on the horses at the Charles Town track are definitely suspect.

The highway department continues its three times a year attacks on roadside wild flowers: the first when the white daisies are in bloom, with supporting blue chicory; the second when the day lilies flourish, and tickseed and yellow daisies; and the third when chicory, wild sunflower, buttonweed and butterfly weed take over. The highway department also disrupts traffic, building three-lane bridges on two-lane roads and leaving the one-lane bridges on two-lane roads. Larry LeHew, the well digger from Front Royal, is still revered for having dug the well that provides just the right volume of water for Washington, the county seat; just enough to meet the needs of thirst and sewage, but not enough to encourage growth or waste. Larry is looked upon as a kind of Moses who brought water out of rock but without subsequently imposing commandments.

A Note to Previous Readers
Reprise

THE FOLLOWING PIECE is taken from the first volume of *The View from Rappahannock*. Those who know the county or have read the earlier book, may skip this essay. Those who have not done either may find this useful information, preparatory to reading more about Rappahannock.

Further into this volume, in the section on local fauna, there are two other repeats from *The View from Rappahannock I*. Included by popular demand (or suspicion that such demand exists) are two essays, one on groundhogs, and one on James Kilpatrick and his problems as a columnist, as a nature lover, and as a resident of the county.

Geography and History

The Lay and Lore of the Land

RAPPAHANNOCK COUNTY, one might say, is a reborn county; it first came into existence in Colonial times, in 1656, when it was split off from Lancaster Shire. It was named after an Indian tribe and lay in the northern neck of Virginia between the Potomac and the Rappahannock Rivers. The first Rappahannock County lost its identity in 1692 when it was divided into Richmond County and Essex County. In 1749 Essex County produced Culpeper County. In turn Culpeper County was divided by The General Assembly of Virginia in 1833 into Rappahannock County and Culpeper County. This division took place despite the objections of the parent county, which may explain a continuing disposition on the part of Culpeper residents and the Culpeper press to downgrade Rappahannock County and its citizens.

The county lies to the east of the Blue Ridge Mountains. Its boundaries were described well in the original petition for separation from Culpeper County in the 1830s. "Beginning at the corner of Madison and Culpeper Counties upon the top of the Blue Ridge Mountains and running thence with the ridge to the beginning."

One of the strong arguments for separation was that "justice removed by 30 or 40 miles" is likely to be "justice denied."

As it now exists Rappahannock County is roughly diamond shaped with the top point at northwest and the lower point at southeast. To its west and northwest, on the other side of the Blue Ridge, lie Warren County and Page County. To the northeast, across the Rappahannock River, lies Fauquier County; to the southwest across Hugh's River lies Madison County; on the southeast line is Culpeper County, separated from Rappahannock by neither mountain nor stream, but by a kind of continuing antagonism.

The terrain of the county is rough and broken. It flows down from the great hollows of the Blue Ridge and from lesser hollows and foothills towards the flatter lands of Virginia to the east.

The Rappahannock River, and Hugh's, which flows into it, are fed by small creeks and runs, such as Indian Run, Hittle's Creek, the Jordan River, Blackwater Run, Hunger Run and White's Run, Beaver Dam Run, Rush River and Hazel River, the Thornton, the Covington, and other waterways of lesser importance.

The economic life of the county rests primarily on cattle raising, on hay, and on fruit crops, principally apples, with some support from peaches, nectarines, and of recent development, vineyards. Forest products also make a modest contribution to the economy of the county. Industries that once flourished are largely gone, including apple processing, with major buildings used for such purposes now abandoned or given over to other uses, one, for example, housing the Rappahannock County Co-op, and another providing cover for antique and craft dealers. Milling, a major industry of the county for years, when as many as 70 mills, it is believed, once operated (grist, flour, and saw mills predominating), is gone from the county.

Two service industries, if they can be called such, remain active in the county: one is religion, the other postal service. County records identify nearly 50 churches, either as operating today, or as having been functional parts of the religious culture of the county. Most were and are Baptist, with Methodist and Episcopal churches also running strongly. Quakers, Catholics, and other denominations have minimal representation. The population, slightly over 5,000, is largely of English ancestry. Currently the number of post offices in the county is nine, or one for every six-to seven-hundred persons. The number of offices that have existed comes very close to forty. As in other parts of Virginia, the small county post office has held out strongly in Rappahannock County, in large part because of the efforts of Senator Harry Byrd, Senior, who although he was for efficiency and economy, generally

U.S. Post Office, Woodville, Virginia

made an exception for the small country offices, which he saw as reminders of government, centers for gathering, and incidentally also politically useful.

While the mills of Rappahannock County ground grist coarse, and the churches ground the spirit exceedingly fine, as God's mills are reputed to do, the post offices refined the politics of the state of Virginia.

Rappahannock County is 75 miles from Washington, D.C., just beyond commuter range, and only marginally within range of Washington's television stations. It does not have cable television, and the number of dishes for picking up satellite programs is small. Moreover, the number of subscribers to the *Washington Post* are few, principally, it seems, because the problem of waste disposal is a difficult one in the county. I cut down my own trips to the trash disposal center from three trips a month to one trip, by canceling my subscription to the *Post* when I found that two-thirds of my trash, by volume, was made up of the newspaper. Subscribers to *The New York Times* are fewer in number than those who subscribe to the *Post*.

Apart from, or in addition to, the fact of geographical protection and cultural insulation, the citizens of Rappahannock County are by nature and history independent. This independence was shown most strongly at the time of the War between the States, when loyalty to the South on the part of Rappahannock was at best marginal. The citizens of the county have maintained this reputation of independence, despite a modest influx of retired military personnel, mostly former colonels, of newspaper persons and media persons, retired, fired, and active, airline pilots and flight attendants and others from the outside. Some proper Virginians refer to Rappahannock County as the Free State of Rappahannock. The county went strongly for Al Smith in 1928, although it had few Catholics and remains today a county without a liquor store, although Smith ran as a "wet."

Cemeteries

Plastic Roses in the Snow

IT CANNOT BE SAID of Rappahannock County, as can be said of the earth, that there are now more persons living on it than have lived on it during all of its previous existence. There are more persons who have lived in Rappahannock County, died, and been buried there than there are in the current population. Cemeteries are given serious attention in the county. Adjacent to most older houses, or marking where such houses once stood, are small cemeteries, some still well maintained, enclosed within stone walls, some with rail fences, and some with wire. Some have been kept free and clear of trees. Some overgrown and marked by thickets of sumac, of locust, of sassafras, or hemlock. A few are marked by ancient oaks and cedars. Of later age and varying condition, are cemeteries adjacent to old churches with graves marked by weather worn limestone markers, some in their leaning defying gravity. Names and dates of birth and death are still legible on some but faded beyond perception on others. In churches still active, at least for burials, granite markers stand among or adjacent to the limestone and marble. Graveyards remain in use, even when churches are closed or gone, like that of the Episcopal Church in Woodville that was destroyed by a tornado years ago and never rebuilt. It seems to be an ecumenical cemetery, possibly accepting the remains of Catholic dead who otherwise might be buried in Culpeper, or in other Catholic burying grounds, or in military cemeteries if they qualify for military burial.

There are community burial grounds, most notably in Flint Hill and Sperryville. Flint Hill bans the placing of plastic flowers, except from November 1 to March 31.

Sperryville has no such limitations, and plastic shows on that hillside place in all seasons—plastic roses in the snow of December, unfading daffodils in the autumn, and again, against the green of spring, mixed with flowers brought from garden and from pot. Easter lilies that will stay on unchanged until September, and occasionally the quiet, unchanging peace is marked by a spinning sunflower turning on its wooden stem. Then again late in the year come the plastic roses in the snow to show the men who roll the eighteen-wheelers down Route 522, that someone remembers and is true.

Fences

From Robert Frost to Paul Mellon

FENCES COME in great variety of materials, form, and purpose. Good fences may not be quite enough to make good neighbors here, as Robert Frost said they do, or did, in Vermont and in New Hampshire. But bad fences, here, certainly make neighbors unhappy. This is especially true if a bull gets through one to heifers not yet ready to be bred, or an unregistered bull intrudes upon a herd of pure-bred cows.

The most respected fence in the county is stone, full height, standing without help of mortar, unaided by boards, posts, or wire. It tells of hard work in clearing fields of rock, of careful building and rebuilding over many years.

Not far below in rank is the half-stone fence, topped by a rail supported by crossed posts or by a post-supported board or two, possibly fortified by hidden wire and with a strand of barbed wire allowed along the top. These are known as "Middleburg" fences or Mellon or Rockefeller fences.

Next in generic ranking of fences are those of wood; of rails, and boards, and wooden posts. In this class the species ranked first is the worm fence, with oak rails, supported by crossed posts, mainly of oak, not sunk in the ground. These are now largely ornamental or ceremonial marking the lines and limits of old battle fields. A new form of worm fence invented recently by Donnie Keyser, a neighbor, is made of mountain locust rails, laid rail on rail, six deep with crossing ends, and nailed with spikes when not yet dry, six rails in height and sure to last a lifetime.

The most common rail fence, and most used, is the "two post" fence laid in straight lines, with two posts, at measured intervals, bound with wire, sustaining oak rails, some new cut, but most reborn from an earlier fence life. The posts may be of locust, or of treated woods, and the rails aided by a strand or two of barbed wire.

One may see occasionally a fence with rails or poles cut and set in holes in posts, but such fences need not be taken seriously by fence watchers, as usually they enclose no more than grass, and trees, and shrubs, and people.

Board fences are fairly standardized as to material, purpose, and style, with slight variations. They are practical fences, used for yards, small plots, and pens, and pastures. They serve well for horses, and for all breeds of cattle. The posts are usually split locust or treated cedar, the boards of oak, nailed, in orders of three or four to the posts. Some fence builders choose to nail the boards on the inside of the posts, a reasonable choice since cattle push from that side. Others nail the boards on the outside of the posts, and some cover the joined boards with a board running vertically at each post, for strength and also for appearance's sake. Practical fence men say there is no good reason for this way of building fences.

A few board fences, usually of short length, are painted white, but most are treated, sprayed or painted, showing black. Some fencers, cattlemen, not concerned with appearance, but with service, and not raising cattle to outdo the income tax collector, leave both oak and locust unpainted, letting nature have its way.

The third group of fences given place and recognition are of wire, at the lowest level simple barbed wire with as many as four strands, generally frowned upon, except as supplemental to other fences, but tolerated in what may qualify as a temporary fence (not quite as temporary as a single strand electrified fence) around a field in soil bank, or a hayfield, or an orchard for post-season grazing. The wire fence most commonly used by those who practice some form of agriculture or livestock raising or feeding, for a livelihood, if not for profit, is a basic fence of woven wire, topped by one or two strands of barbed wire, sustained by posts of varying kind, with locust or cedar as a rule, sometimes with lesser posts of steel, or spindly locust set between the heavier posts. Such fences are all-purpose. They will hold horses, cows, sheep, and even swine. Some fence builders prefer a narrow roll of woven wire with space below it for one strand of barbed wire, the easier to do battle with honeysuckle, the major enemy of fences in the county.

And then there is the prince of woven wire fences, for horse farms, of the highest order, triangularly woven, guaranteed proof against any horse's folly, and with one board at the top to protect the head and neck of thoroughbreds.

There is one other fence of late introduction, unproved and therefore not generally approved: a high-tension fence, with smooth wire running free in staples or eyes, infrequent solid posts, with spreaders in between, and provision for electric help, to hold disrespectful cows.

Beyond the accepted posts, and strands, and boards and rails, are the fences of the shiftless: a mixed lot, somewhat like the cattle they attempt to hold, parts of old stone fences, or of old rail fences, with interweavings of woven or barbed wire, fastened to whatever is available, downed trees, and standing ones, steel posts, pipes, parts of iron beds. Fences, local experts say, can, if you study them carefully, tell a lot about the character of farm owners, their wives, their economic status (real or desired, improving or declining), major sources of income, kind and value of horses or cattle being pastured, regard or disregard for neighbors, for wildlife, especially for quail, for nature (honeysuckle, trumpet vine, brambles, dogwood, hawthorn, or any combination of the above). A board fence, with faded and flaked paint and some broken boards, usually indicates that the farm or its owner once knew better days. A pasture with economically and socially more acceptable fencing, say rail or board, on the front or road-facing line, and lesser fencing on side or back sides, indicates concern for social acceptance rather than concern for economic realities. Farms with extended board fences enclosing a whole pasture of some size, are usually marked as being supported, directly or indirectly, immediately or remotely, by revenue derived from sources other than the current farming operation, either inheritance or income tax avoidance. Character and social aspirations of wives, too, can be read into quality of fences and into painting and treatment of fencing. Fences broken down and loaded with honeysuckle are usually read as signs of surrender whereas those with hedge roses and brambles may indicate a friendship for quail. Some experts can easily tell, they claim, what kind of cattle the fence was built for (or what kind of horses and sheep). They also distinguish among breeds of cattle, Angus requiring the tightest fence. Nothing in the county is ever quite as simple as it seems.

Merkles

Merkles

Moments of Truth

FOR EIGHT YEARS, on and off, since moving to Rappahannock County come April, I have been hunting "merkles," the morels of this area. Each season was marked by progressive disappointment and disillusionment with both the merkle and the merkle hunters, until I was very close to giving up on the quest. It was not that I hadn't tried.

I had searched for merkles at random. I had consulted experienced merkle gatherers, following the advice of some who said one should search the south side of ridges, others, the north side, and a few who recommended the west slope or the east, depending on the time of the day. I took the recommendations of those who said one should look near the base of poplar trees, and of those who said the best place for merkle growth was around the stumps of hard pines or in abandoned apple orchards or, as a few advisors suggested, around oak trees.

I accepted gifts of a few merkles, pleading that I or a friend had never tasted them. I elicited promises from merkle hunters that come the next season they would take me with them. Some promised, but until last year no one had fulfilled the promise.

Meanwhile I continued my own efforts using more scientific and more subtle methods. Having heard that blue-eyed persons have more success in finding merkles, I invited my neighbor Dennis Fairbrother to come with me. He has blue eyes. He brought his two-year-old daughter who also has blue eyes. I welcomed her, believing that innocence might be a condition to successful merkle hunting, as it is, or was, in finding the unicorn. He brought with him three brown-eyed Golden Retrievers. I brought my Australian Shepherd, which had one brown eye and one blue eye.

We attended Easter Sunrise Service on Red Oak Mountain preliminary to our search. There were three preachers, each one of whom in his remarks made reference to the certainty of the sunrise, of the coming of spring, of the blossoming of the redbud and of the wild cherry trees, and of other promises of spring that had been fulfilled or would be. I waited for some promise relative to merkles. There was none.

At the post-sunrise service breakfast, half way down Red Oak Mountain, I managed to turn the talk to merkles. Tom Massie responded immediately. I had never looked upon Tom as a merkle expert. I had never seen him wearing the right kind of cap. I knew that he was a fairly good tennis player, especially in mixed doubles, if he had a good partner. He dressed well. I assumed that he was a good horseman, but had never associated him with merkles. I may have been wrong. At the mention of the word merkle, Tom became animated. He told of his successes in finding merkles, reporting that he had once collected half a trash-bag of merkles. As he reported his achievements, he turned occasionally to his son for verification. The son said nothing, but seemed to endorse what his father had said. I thought of asking Tom's wife for a supporting statement, but for two reasons did not do so. First, because as a general rule, I never question what merkle hunters say and, second, because of the long-standing rule that a wife cannot be called upon to testify against her husband. Moreover, Tom Massie does, I had noted, have the blue eyes of a true merkle hunter.

I was somewhat indifferent to the approach of the 1987 season. One Saturday early in April (ahead of time, I thought) I saw the usual sign of merkle hunter activity, a pickup truck parked marginally off Route 618, near a mountain ridge reputed to bear merkles. The width of Route 618 is such that one can park only marginally. That was a Saturday; I saw no hunter leaving the hill that day, but on Sunday in a casual walk, I met three searchers returning to their car. They were carrying paper bags, carefully, a sign that they had had some success. I told them, truthfully, that I had a visitor who had never seen merkles, and wondered if they could spare a sample or two. I was given one merkle. This limited generosity was comparable to what had been shown me in previous seasons. I was ready to conclude that all was as it had been in other years. I was wrong. . .

On the next weekend, on Saturday, in my absence, someone left me not one merkle, but a quart or more, in a sack at my doorway with no identification. This seemed strange behavior. More was to follow. On Sunday I received a call from Tom Massie. My confidence and trust in Tom had begun to fade, but on this Easter day it was restored. He did take me with him into the mountains. The merkles were there in great abundance, as one measures abundance of merkles. I had previously found under instruction a few merkles in old apple orchards, but never before made a true wood's find.

I returned to my house with merkles enough to give to a neighbor, who in earlier years had accompanied me on unsuccessful forays into our woods.

Even more was to come. On the next weekend I received a call from a person in Peola Mills who, remembering my sad story of previous years, recalling my despair of ever finding merkles, wanted to tell me that I was welcome to come pick merkles ("not all," she said) that were growing under a wild crab apple tree, the location of which she offered to give me. I thanked her, and asked to be remembered another year, and reported my satisfying success on the previous weekend, adding that I had even given some merkles away.

I am not yet ready to believe that merkle hunters can always be counted on to be sharing and generous under all circumstances and all seasons, but have revised the judgment that was growing to be almost absolute because of my experience with them in years past, that they were all unreliable—not quite untruthful, but lacking in generosity and a sense of sharing.

My opinion now is that there comes a point at which a merkle hunter who is successful in his hunt is moved to what at least appears to be generosity, both in sharing his knowledge of places where the mushrooms do grow, and beyond that sharing what is found. But that point is not easily defined or predicted. In the dealing with merkles, I believe, a person must reach a point like that of the "critical mass" of nuclear materials, when something drastic happens—explosions, in the case of nuclear mass and "truth and generosity" in the case of the merkle hunter.

Next year's merkle season, I expect, will be different from this one, and from all that have gone before. After observing six merkle seasons carefully and scientifically, and studying the character and habits of merkle hunters, I have concluded that no two merkle seasons are alike, and that no two merkle hunters or gatherers are the same, and even that the same person as a merkle hunter changes from season to season.

From Merkle Hunting to Turkey Calling

. . .and Back

HAVING HAD IN THE SPRING OF 1987, after many such seasons of trying, great success in finding merkles, I relaxed, believing that I had passed the ultimate Rappahannock County test of dedication, concentration, and perseverance and that I could rest on my laurels, or merkles.

It was not to be so. One morning in the country store, I learned that merkle finding was not the ultimate test, but merely the penultimate one and that the real, absolute test for all of the virtues required in the pursuit of merkles is turkey calling. Having had my peace of mind disturbed by this information, I suggested that maybe handling coon hounds might be a more demanding test than either merkle hunting or turkey calling. This suggestion was rejected as in no way comparable, by the local experts.

I had been a casual turkey caller for some ten years, using as my instrument a Lynch's Fool Proof Turkey Call, Model 101, which a friend had given to me. As a rule I worked from the comfort of a lawn chair, and only after I had heard a turkey on Jubal Mountain, which is behind my house, or on Turkey Mountain, a ridge that lies across the road from my house. I thought I got responses, although I never drew a gobbler into the clearing around my house. One February morning, without my calling, some thirty turkeys did come within twenty feet of my bedroom window to feed on the berries of a dogwood tree. I assumed that my summer and autumn calls had had a subliminal effect. My principal doubt about the efficacy of my calls was that often they were answered not by turkeys but by crows.

In any case, I decided to take up the challenge of turkey calling, to talk to local experts and to read what was available on the science or the art of turkey calling.

As a part of my decision I resolved first to concentrate on the call I owned. I reread the instructions on how to use it, and also the claims as to what could be done with it, and set out to master the yelp, cluck, put, whine, and cackle, all of which the box claimed it was capable of producing.

I had a few doubts about my box. First I wondered about why the box was said to be "fool proof." Was it, I wondered, proof against the caller or the callee, the person or the turkey? If the words applied to the latter, it seemed to me that the user of the device was doomed to defeat.

I wondered, too, about the model number 101. Had Lynch tested one hundred models before developing this one, somewhat in the way that the U.S. Air Force had gone through a numbered series of bombers, including those of special note, the B17, the B19, the B52, and finally a B71, after which for some reason the Air Force started over, with the B1 of current use even though it has been crashing too frequently and some experts say that it is not only unsafe but obsolete. It is to be replaced by a new plane, the B2, of the second series of numbers, also known as the "stealth bomber."

Possibly Lynch has a new model on the drawing board (if not in production), a more subtle one. For the immediate use, the Lynch Model 101 seemed to be a reasonably advanced and sophisticated instrument. The sounding box appeared to be oak, a good wood, and the scraper or bow of pine. My confidence in the Lynch call was soon shaken. Again on a Sunday morning, in the country store, I raised what I thought were subtle questions about calling turkeys and turkey calls. I mentioned my Lynch model, only to have a man in a camouflage suit advise me that the 101 was a primitive instrument. He said that he was an experienced turkey hunter. I had some doubts about his claims to being a turkey hunter since he was wearing the camouflage suit. Turkeys, it is generally believed, are color blind and are as alert to a moving camouflaged hunter as they are to one who is wearing red or orange. Some experts hold that wearing the warning colors is likely to save one from being shot for a turkey, especially if one is a good caller. The camouflaged self-described hunter, after asking me to wait, rushed out to his pick-up truck to return with what he said was the top of the line in box calls, a veritable Stradivarius. The box, he pointed out to me, was laminated, alternating imported mahogany with native Virginia walnut, with the bow, or scraper, of walnut, to be drawn across the leading box edge of mahogany. My confidence in the Lynch call was shaken, and I began to look about for other calls.

Since I could find nothing in the market comparable to the laminated model I had been shown in the store, I looked to other types of calls. I soon found two calls, the first a variation on the Lynch model, with a sounding board and box of cherry wood, activated by a chalked wooden rod. The sound I was able to draw from this instrument was little different from that which I had been getting from Lynch. My second added call was technically quite different from the other two. It was called "the echo turkey call," the invention of Don Murray of Boston, Virginia. Its central part was a rubber diaphragm, to be inserted into the top of the caller's mouth, and activated according to the following instructions: the user is to put the call on his tongue, about half way back (that is half a tongue) with the rounded side up, and the open end (the call is horseshoe shaped) pointing toward the front teeth. Then he is told to push the device up into the roof of the mouth, hold a little pressure on the rubber center with the tongue, and huff (note well, not puff) from the chest. If the huffed air goes over the top of the call without producing any sound, it may be necessary to trim the tape edges of the call. Evidently this adjustment depends on the shape of the user's mouth. The user is told that he should not expect success unless the seal tape surrounding the diaphragm is tight. The manufacturer makes no recommendation for the use of Polygrip but warns the user to keep the tongue on the rubber diaphragm as he huffs from the chest until some sound is made.

The first sound may well be a squeal or some form of whistle, the user is told. After getting the primal squeal or whistle the huffer should strive to get a continuous shrill sound, and then by dropping the tongue in rhythm with one's huffing, produce the basic turkey call, the "yelp."

This turkey call comes in a plastic container, sealed like photographic film, with advice that the instrument should be kept in a cool, dark place, if not used for long periods of time; that the owner should air dry the diaphragm and then store it in its plastic box, wrapped in aluminum foil, in a refrigerator. Owners are also advised to avoid bending the frame of the diaphragm, and that if they are not completely satisfied, to call or write the inventor and distributor, Don Murray.

The instructions alone were enough to dissuade me even from testing the Echo call, and I gave thought to trying to find another type of turkey call I had learned of, one made from the hollow wing bone of a turkey, and thought of trying the mouthpiece of my clarinet, when I read an article on turkey hunting, calling, and calls in the magazine *Virginia Wildlife*. That article may have saved me from a lifetime of turkey calling. From it I learned that in the opinion of some turkey hunters, calling is much less effective now than it was in the past. The reasons given for the unresponsiveness varied from expert to expert, one holding that calling is less effective because there are more turkey hens available and therefore there is no need for gobbling. Another holds that there are too many hunters and too many turkey callers. One expert holds that the quality and tone of the call is important, another that the sound is all but irrelevant, that what is important is the rhythm of the call. "Every turkey," he holds, "has the same rhythm."

I have decided that until there is more agreement among the experts that I will put off my turkey calling project, and settle, at least for the time being, for the penultimate success, if that is what it is, that goes with successful merkle hunting.

Where Have All the Bluebirds Gone?

And Why?

ACCORDING TO JOYCE KELLY, president of the Defenders of Wildlife, a number of nongame species of birds, including loons, barn owls, wood storks, and bluebirds are "under pressure," and because of loss of habitat and other threats are declining in numbers. My concern for the loons, the barn owls, and the wood storks was immediately stirred. But as to the bluebirds, I had some reservations.

I have tried to help bluebirds. They have been unresponsive to my efforts, spurning a variety of houses that I have offered for their comfort, convenience, and safety.

First I provided a standard bluebird house, built by ornithologist and woodworker Thomas Gheoghan of Scrabble, Virginia. The entrance hole was exactly the right size to let in bluebirds but keep out starlings and other intruders. The hole was placed the prescribed five inches above the floor of the house. The roof was hinged so as to make it easier to remove undesirable tenants such as house sparrows. The house was fixed on the side of a locust tree. It was eight feet from the ground and fastened to the side of the tree that opened on the edge of a meadow. Anti-blacksnake protection was provided. Although the house has been available for three years, no bluebird has moved in.

I offered more sophisticated housing; two houses, in fact, that were given to me by friends, miniature models of the White House, on the assumption that that house is attractive to birds of many kinds. I chose suitable locations for the houses, one atop a fence post and the other in an apple tree.

The house in the apple tree remains unoccupied after two summers. I once saw a wren examine it critically and then leave. Not even a sparrow has deigned to move into it. The other house has drawn the attention of a flicker which set out to remodel it by enlarging the entrance hole. Evidently after getting a look inside, the flicker abandoned the move. Birds may not be political.

Finally, I went modern with a ceramic house, designed by an artist and shaped like a gourd. A wren has moved in and occupied the designer house for two seasons, but the bluebirds, for whom it was designed, have ignored it.

Although I continued to see bluebirds, I took some consolation from reports that the number of bluebirds was significantly reduced. If this was the case, my failure to attract them could be attributed to trends and general conditions rather than personal inadequacy.

The number might be declining because, as the experts were saying, much of their natural habitat was being destroyed by conversion of rural areas into suburban areas. I could understand why any self-respecting species of bird would not tolerate a suburb. But Rappahannock County is not suburban. Starlings might be taking breeding sites away from bluebirds, as some experts said, but there are few starlings in Rappanhannock County.

Insecticides, undoubtedly, were having some effect. Yet doubts remained. I continued to see blue flashes along the roads and in fields, and pastures—bluebirds in flight as though trying to fly out of their color.

I began to doubt the experts. Maybe the numbers were not down. Maybe the bluebirds were hiding, or flying so fast they can scarcely be seen or counted. What could be the cause?

I think I have found the answer in Ms. Kelly's report, from which I learned that whereas there were only 15.9 million Americans who hunted wild game in 1985, there were 93 million bird watchers and wildlife photographers loose in the country that same year.

Bird watchers dress strangely and move in unusual ways, not like animals or other human beings. Their hats and caps are especially peculiar. Most of them, I know, carry field glasses and use cameras. The lenses of all these devices must flash in the sun as they are turned on birds. The cameras click and whir, and some of them flash.

Bluebirds are not secretive, nor are they recluses, but they do like marginal privacy. Ninety-three million bird watchers on the loose may well have driven the bluebirds to more secluded and protected places, where they continue to increase and multiply, I hope.

Neither Love, Nor War

Chicken Neutrality

IT WAS WITH RELIEF that I read a recent scientific report from Virginia Tech. According to the report, Dr. Alvin Leighton, a poultry science professor at that institution, has discovered what seems to be an important fact about the behavior patterns of chickens and turkeys; namely, that longer wave lengths of light, that is, the red and yellow on the light spectrum, stimulate the eyes of chickens and turkeys, and by passing through the eyes, trigger the hypothalamus, which, in turn, sends a message to the pituitary gland to release hormones to begin the reproductive cycle.

The scientist has concluded that if the red and yellow wave-lengths, somehow, could be kept from passing through the eyes or reaching them, the hormones that start the reproductive cycle would not be released, and that if these reproductive urges were controlled, reduced in strength, or eliminated altogether, the birds, both male and female, would be more docile, less agitated. The hens in contentment would lay more eggs, and both male and female birds, undisturbed by sexual drives, would eat quietly and utilize feed more efficiently, largely because they would spend less time fighting each other—even to the point that the tendency of chickens, under some circumstamances, to peck each other to death would be moderated.

All of these good things, good in the judgment of the scientist (the chickens and roosters, the hen and tom turkeys were not consulted), could be achieved if the chickens and the turkeys were fitted with contact lenses that would screen out the dangerous and stimulating rays.

What is interesting in the report is not so much its potential for increasing the production of chicken and turkey meat and eggs, desirable as these ends may be, but that the report gives scientific suport to a method used in handling chickens some 40 years ago. In those days, nearly every farm had a small flock of chickens. Most eggs were fertilized and had to be checked before they were eaten. Chicks were hatched by setting hens, and roosters fought regularly. The most serious problem of handling chickens arose during the winter months when, because of cold weather, it was necessary to house chickens in relatively small coops. In close quarters it was not uncommon for chickens to peck a weak chicken to death. As the Virginia study notes, they may still do so at all seasons of the year.

In those simpler days farmers did the best they could. They thought about the problem and concluded that it was the blood on a chicken, accidentally wounded or struck by a vicious peck by another chicken or rooster, that attracted the flock. Farmers reasoned, or concluded, that if chickens could not see the blood on the wounded bird they would not peck or pick on it. The next step was to seek a way of concealing the blood from the cannibalistic flock. Again the chicken farmers, or at least one of them, thought about the problem and concluded that the thing to do was to paint the windows of the chicken coop red, or rose-colored, so that chickens would see the world through rose- painted glass—or better—to install red or rose-colored glass and put in rose-tinted light bulbs.

The procedure seemed to work despite the word of scientists of the time that chickens were color-blind. It may well be that Professor Leighton has found the answer, and that, although done for the wrong scientific reason, the painting of the window panes and the coloring of the light bulbs, may have accomplished what the rose-tinted contact lenses are designed to do.

Dr. Leighton's findings may have important application to the human beings who, fitted with rose-tinted lenses, may be less irritable, and even less warlike.

The Guns of June and July

Groundhog Days

IN THREE YEARS OF RESIDENCE in Rappahannock County, I found that persons living in the county, and especially those living in the area of Scrabble and Hawlin Hollow, had a deep respect and love for all animals, both domestic and wild.

They were not overly sentimental. They acknowledged the laws of nature, accepting that hawks would prey on field mice and on lesser birds; that foxes would eat moles and rabbits and occasionally, a chicken; that raccoons would eat frogs, birds' eggs, and other things; that skunks had a right to life, along with opossum, chipmunks, and squirrels.

They would use animals against animals in civilized ways: fox hounds to chase the fox, coon hounds to pursue the wily raccoon. They rode horses. They hunted deer, quail, wild turkey—even bears—in season. Poachers were not socially approved.

Among all of these considerate and animal-loving people, three were outstanding: one, a journalist, writer, especially partial to Collies of any size or color but to all other animals, I thought, understanding and friendly. He had written a book about the wonders of animals and maintained the best bird feeders in the county.

The second was a semi-retired professor, a gentle person, a lover of animals. He fed birds and chipmunks, put salt out for deer, maintained oak trees for squirrels and even an old hollow, unsightly basswood tree for bees.

The third was an airplane pilot, sustained in his love of animals by his wife. Together they kept three Golden Retrievers who retrieved only tennis balls and Frisbees. They supported two horses, which they never rode. They had a tom cat, blind in one eye, who spent one third of his time in the veterinary hospital, one third of his time away from home, and one third of his time patrolling the house, holding the mice at bay as his mistress refused to use traps or poison. They had, for a time, four geese. When two of them disappeared just before Christmas and two at Easter time, rather than believe the obvious that the geese had been taken by foxes, leaving no trace of feathers, they accused two of their most trustworthy neighbors of having stolen the geese.

Thus man and nature seemed in perfect harmony, in Hawlin Hollow and Scrabble, until one night at the journalist's house when the talk turned to dogs; I entered the conversation, speaking for my Australian Shepherd. She had not proved herself in handling sheep or cattle, I admitted, but she did have a potent herding instinct and was most gentle with animals, I said.

"Only yesterday evening," I reported innocently, "I heard her barking in the yard. I went out to see her herding a young groundhog very carefully until it climbed into the lower branches of a small magnolia tree. At which point the dog, apparently believing that she had accomplished her mission, abandoned the groundhog in the tree."

I stopped, waiting for approval. None came. There was a pause, then the journalist asked, in what I considered a suspicious tone, "What did you do with the groundhog?"

"Well," I said, "I put the dog in the house, took a broom, poked the animal out of the tree, and chased it off into the woods."

There was a shocked silence. Neighbor looked at neighbor. I was puzzled. I asked myself had I offended someone or someone's dog, or abused a groundhog?

In Minnesota, my home state, groundhogs are of minimal interest and are seldom mentioned excepting as weather prophets on or about February 2nd. I recalled having seen dead groundhogs, tied by their tails, hanging from the branches of trees along country roads in Rappahannock County. I waited in a state of mild apprehension.

The author of the animal-loving book finally broke silence.

"You let the groundhog get away!" he exclaimed. "Why didn't you kill it?"

"I don't have a gun," I responded.

"Then why didn't you use a club? Do you know what you have let loose in this county?" he continued. "That one groundhog in its lifetime can dig enough holes in pastures and in fields to cause ten or fifteen horses to fall and break their legs. Riders will be crippled, possibly killed. That one groundhog and its progeny will destroy hundreds of pounds of garden crops and acres of sweet corn."

"You," he concluded, "had a groundhog treed and let it go, when I spend days lying in wait for one to show up near my garden."

"Groundhogs," he added, and he is a religious man, "should never have been allowed on the Ark."

I left the party early.

The next morning, as I was driving into town to pick up my mail, I approached the house of the college professor. As I neared the house I saw the gentle professor, or so I thought him to be, coming down the road. He was wearing sneakers and socks, shorts and shirt, and a kind of baseball cap, his usual attire for his daily walk. But today he was not walking. He was moving in a stalking crouch, and carrying a rifle.

I slowed to a stop as I reached him. "What's wrong, professor?" I asked.

He looked up at me from his crouched position. His eyes were bright with a light I had never seen in them before. "Groundhog," he hissed. "Keep going."

I went on and got my mail. On my return I stopped to see how the professor was. He had returned from the hunt and was sitting quietly on his front porch drinking lemonade. The strange light had gone out of his eyes. I ventured to ask him about the gorundhog. "Dead," he said. "I got him with one shot." He then went on to tell me that in his life time he had killed more than one hundred groundhogs, and that he hoped to increase the number greatly now that he had more time.

Later in that same week, on an afternoon walk, I stopped to visit the airline pilot and his wife. On being admitted to the kitchen, the first thing I noticed was a 30-30 rifle leaning against the kitchen stove.

I had never seen a gun in the house before.

"What's the gun for?" I asked.

"What for?" the pilot responded. "What else but for shooting groundhogs?"

"Your wife won't let you shoot them, will she?" I asked. I had seen her cry when the pigs were slaughtered in the early spring.

"She loads the gun," her husband replied.

I called my gentle dog up from under the table, got safely through the three Golden Retrievers that were guarding the kitchen door, and headed for home.

As I walked down the lane, I could hear behind me the sound of gunfire echoing through the hollow.

Mollie

R.I.P.

MY DOG "MOLLIE" spent the best days of her life in Rappahannock County; irregularly, a few days or a week at a time between her second and fourth years; and then with a permanent address, and residence, interrupted by days and weeks in Washington, D.C. until her death in 1988. It was here that she learned what ice is, and groundhogs and bees; met skunks and 'possum, and raccoons; sensed the presence of bobcat and bear; and practiced her herding skills whenever given a chance with children or cows. Once kicked by a horse, she gave up on horses; and outsped by rabbits and deer, she ignored them. After one experience with an electric fence, she would enter pastures only through open gates.

She learned respect for cats, but not for dogs, nor for people who laughed too loudly or waved their arms without purpose or shuffled their feet beneath a table.

Mollie was an Australian Shepherd. Australian Shepherds are an unusual breed, first recognized and registered in the United States some thirty years ago. The breed, or what became "the Breed," was brought here from Australia (where it is believed it picked up some "Dingo" blood) by Basque sheepherders. The dog is mainly of Spanish origin, although there is a school of dog experts, a very limited one, that holds that some of the dog's ancestors were Celtic.

In any case, the Australian Shepherd is no ordinary dog. It is, my dog book states, distinguished by "character and intelligence," rather than color, size or conformation. Its eye colors can be blue, brown, hazel, amber, or any combination, with no order of preference. Mollie had one brown eye and one blue one, the combination I prefer. Her ears were as they should be, not pricked or hanging, but broken about three quarters from the base, indicating a restrained alertness. She was "blue merle." Some Australian Shepherds are born with a natural bobtail. Some have to be docked. Mollie, the record states, was docked.

Australian Shepherd owners (that word must be used with qualification, since an Australian Shepherd can never be wholly owned in the way that most other dogs can be, with accompanying obedience, even subservience) are resigned to the difficulties of showing their dogs. The problem exists at the lower levels of canine competition, the level at which the "best of breed" is determined. Every Australian Shepherd, unlike Australian Cattle dogs, or other breeds such as Beagles and Golden Retrievers, is different from every other Australian Shepherd. Each in its own way, therefore, is "best of breed." An Australian Shepherd owner never has to apologize or defensively admit any deficiency in his or her dog. Owners of Golden Retrievers are quick to say, even without challenge, that their dog's nose is a little too long, or that its color is a little off, or that the dog's hind quarters are not quite right, etc. Somehow, by lot possibly, if an Australian Shepherd could get through the barrier within its own breed and be entered in the contest of "best of show," any Australian Shepherd could win.

Meanwhile the Australian Shepherd waits, remaining true to itself—and resisting the corruption of cross-breeding. One sled dog owner thought that by crossing a sled dog with the Australian Shepherd, noted for its intelligence and endurance, he could develop a super sled dog. His experiment did not work. Australian Shepherds are not meant to pull loads. Even when bred down to one quarter Australian Shepherd, the dogs, although they would keep the traces of the harness taut, would not pull.

Their herding quality, the experimenter reported, remained unchanged and when released at the end of a sled run, they would occasionally herd a moose into camp.

Mollie is gone.

MOLLIE

I know that you will not come back,
Not answer to my call or whistle,
Not come even at your pleasure,
As was your way.
Yet, I will leave your "good dog" pad and dish
Beside the kitchen sink, a while,
Your rawhide bone beneath a chair,
The cans of dog food on the shelf,
Your favorite ball,
Hid in the boxwood hedge.
I'll listen in the early morning light,
For your muted huff, not quite a bark,
Suggesting you be let out.
And lie in half-sleep until
I hear your harp-like,
Single scratch upon the screen,
To signal you had answered nature's call,
Made your accustomed rounds,
Checked the limits of the grounds,
For trace of groundhogs, raccoons, even bears,
And now returned intent on sleep
On bed, or rug, or floor,
Depending on your mood.
And if not answered,
Lie down in silent protest
Against my failure to respond
And to show resentment of the
Indifference of the stolid door.

I will not yet remove
The mist of dog hair
From your favorite chair.
Not yet discard the frazzled frisbee
You could catch, making plays,
Going away, like Willie Mays,
But having proved your skill,
Refused to fetch.
Let retrievers tire themselves
In repetitious runs, you seemed to say.
You would run figure eights,
Disdaining simple circles,
Jump hedges just for sport.
Eat holes in woolen blankets
But leave untouched
The silk or satin bindings.
Herd sheep and cattle,
Spurn running rabbits and deer,
That would not play your game.
You swam with ducks
And walked among wild geese,
Ate Tums but not Rolaids.
You knew no dog-like shame.
And died by no dog's disease at end,
But by one that also lays its claim on men.

The Old White Mare

From Borysthenes to Katie

JIM BILL FLETCHER is a well-known, quite possibly the best-known, lawyer in Rappahannock County. He is also known outside the county, in Richmond, Virginia, even as far away as New York.

For years he was the master of the Rappahannock Hunt and in his best years with the Hunt rode a gray (later white) mare, Katie. Katie still lives, nearing 30 years of age.

The poem was written to honor Jim Bill Fletcher at a recent birthday celebration, and turned out better than I had expected, when accidentally or providentially as I was working at it, I read in a history of ancient hunting the story of the Emperor Hadrian's hunting horse, Borysthenes (translate, the Nomad), and of his death and burial as reported on his epitaph.

BORYSTHENES AND KATIE

"Jim Bill will bury that horse," said Clifton Clark
Of Katie, the old white mare.
No one in the country store did dare
Question or challenge Clifton's remark.

"She'll never be trucked to a slaughter house
To be shot, and skinned, and ground into meal,
Or having died a natural death, to a rendering plant,
To be boiled, and melted and distilled
To the essence of horse and beyond.
She'll not be fed to the hounds in the kennel

Or stripped of her hide and left in the pasture
For hogs and vultures and crows.
She'll not be cremated with brush fire and oil
Nor stuffed, moth-proofed and hung on a frame
Like Lee's horse, Traveler, of Civil War fame.

A horse like her is hard to find
And not to be treated as ordinary kind.
She never fell, or threw man, woman, or child.
Yet she set the pace for every ride.
She would jump what other horses refused,
But none but a fool, horse or man,
Would try when she turned aside."

She'll be buried there on the west hillside
Whole of body, with unmarked hide
Not crowded or jammed in a ditch,
But laid on her side in an ample grave,
Neck extended, legs stretched for a joyful run
With Borysthenes, Hadrian's hunter
Who some 2000 years ago, his epitaph states,

"Galloped through plains
And marshy meadows
Past old Etruscan barrows
And chased the Pannonian boars."
"Lived long, and then
With his legs unblemished
Met his fate, appointed,
And in the field was buried."

Trouble in Scrabble

Sage and Skunk

AS A RULE one should never go to the aid of a columnist in distress. Columnists in trouble should be left, at least, for a few weeks, "turning slowly in the wind," the treatment recommended for his enemies by Richard Nixon or one of his aides.

I am breaking this rule in the case of columnist James, locally known as "Jack" Kilpatrick of Scrabble, Virginia. Jack, as we all know in Rappahannock County, is a noted columnist, commentator, speaker, and writer. He has been an editor. The range of his interests and of his knowledge is extensive. In the course of one week's work, he has been known to give near absolute judgments on problems ranging from how to settle the continuing crisis in the Middle East (one that has been in progress for approximately 4,000 years); and the problem of Northern Ireland, which is itself about 70 years old but is a part of a conflict of much longer duration, approximately the 1,000 years of British interference in the affairs of the Irish; to advise the President on how to control inflation and insure Republican Congressional election victories.

Jack's knowledge is not limited to the world of politics, economics, and social reform. He is an expert also in the realm of nature. He can read storms and seasons. He knows how the moon runs among the branchings of the sun. He can teach weatherlore, and the ways of the wild things. Whereas he is generally sympathetic and humanely disposed to nature's creatures, even those that do harm to his garden and shrubs, he can be hard. He draws the line at groundhogs. If Jack had been consulted in the formulation of the curse put on Adam for his sin, he would surely have suggested, possibly insisted, that to the punishment of the

46

"thorns and thistles" the groundhog should have been added.

Jack has been brought low. If the written word could speak or cry out, there would be crying in the wind in the area adjacent to the Kilpatrick demesne, "White Oak," near Scrabble.

Jack has been brought so low that he is asking the editors of the 450 papers that print his column for help. The profundity of his act of humility can be measured only if one understands that help from editors is the last thing a columnist will accept. In fact the redeeming grace, the distinguishing mark, of a columnist is that he has passed over into that happy state in which he is not subject to editorial review or judgment, either approving or disapproving.

Moreover, having been an editor, Jack Kilpatrick knows how serious it is to ask an editor to stand up from his editor's chair, to come out from behind his editor's desk, to put aside the protection of editorial anonymity, and to speak or write without the covering defense that the views do not "necessarily reflect the opinion of the editors."

What could have brought on this moment of truth? It was a skunk, a female skunk, according to Jack's observation. This female skunk, called Rosebud, has established herself under the Kilpatrick guest cottage and Jack does not know how to get rid of her.

Jack, he admits, has not tried every possible means. Columnists do not have to be pragmatic. They can figure things out through pure speculation. And he has given consideration to riddance methods, ranging from the most violent and primitive means of destruction in keeping with a recommendation in a poem by Yeats for "a bloody and a sudden end," "gunshot, or a noose," to more subtle forms of capital punishment, originally supported by liberal executioners, such as the guillotine, operating on the principle of gravitational pull therefore requiring no commensurate exercise of human strength on the part of the executioner; and poison gas, released by the body heat of the victim. He has even considered inhumane means, either starvation or suffocation by blocking the escape hole with cement blocks.

The more subtle methods of persuasion and of psychology have not been overlooked. Modestly Jack has suggested that his gardener-caretaker undertake this mission.

Although I have long honored the rule not to tread where angels, editors, and columnists fear to tread, and have hesitated to enter some places where the above

Mephitis Mephitis

mentioned do not fear to tread, the desperation of Jack's call for help has moved me to make one suggestion to him, a suggestion based on boyhood experience on a Minnesota farm long ago.

The whole process was called "twisting a skunk." The instrument: a ball of barbed wire, attached to heavier smooth wire, with a handle (a kind of prototype of the modern Roto-Rooter).

The technique was to insert the ball-end of the instrument into the skunk's den and then slowly rotate it, by twisting at the far end of the wire handle, until the operator sensed some engagement of the barbed wire and the skunk. The compelling principle is that a skunk under challenge or stress will turn tail, but not run from whatever threatens it. The skunk's tail becomes involved in the ball of barbed wire. When fully engaged, that is, the tail and the skunk with its tail immobilized in the wire entanglement, the skunk is slowly drawn from the hole and then disposed of humanely or otherwise.

Whereas, as every columnist knows, and most have said, when in need of a metaphor, a tail wagging a dog is an undesirable relationship; a tail wagging a skunk is the best one can hope for under the circumstances.

The Jail, Washington, Virginia

County Justice
The Un-Common Law

JURIES AND JUDGES in the county are not quick to find persons guilty. There are no judges generally noted as harsh or hanging judges. Justice is tempered by experience, common sense, history, a sensitivity to extenuating circumstances, such as passion or property rights. Fence lines and right-of-way are given special respect.

It appeared a few years ago that the administration of justice might be a growth industry in the county. That development seems not to have occurred. The threat of growth came from the disposition of two cases each involving use of fire arms and death.

One case involved horse trainers from a nearby county. One trainer was shot and killed, the other did the shooting. The man charged with murder was acquitted on the grounds that his action was a crime of passion. His wife was involved. It was popularly acknowledged, although this was not an open legal consideration in the trial, that the rules between horse trainers are by tradition different from those that apply to the general population.

The second case, one originating in the county, was more complicated. It involved property, a right-of-way, a bulldozer, a pick-up truck, a woman in the truck armed with a shot gun, against a man in the bulldozer with a rifle and a revolver. The man was killed, the woman acquitted on grounds that she had acted in self-defense.

These were not typical county cases, which are more likely to be like the recurring one involving Eustice Benton Dodson, who has been arrested at irregular intervals over the years for violation of state and possibly federal liquor laws.

Eustice is now in jail or out of jail. It is hard to keep up with his record. If he is out, he probably will soon be charged again with the customary charge of selling illegally liquor which was sold to him legally. In his most celebrated arrest, Eustice was reported to have had a total stock of two opened fifths of Canadian Mist, which the judge ordered destroyed; 39 gallons of whiskey, presumably bourbon; four gallons of wine; and 38 gallons of beer, all of which the judge ordered handed over to the State of Virginia. The judge also imposed on Eustice, who was not in good health, a sentence of 240 days of community service. This penalty was never imposed because, as the county attorney said, there were no community needs in the county that could be served by Eustice.

The whittlers at the Corner Store in Sperryville agreed that what Eustice had been arrested for was probably the best community service he could perform. The whittlers also thought that his arrest was suspect, since the agent who purchased the incriminating liquor had posed as an antique dealer, which is looked upon in the county as a profession, like that of a preacher or minister, which can be trusted and should not be used in scam operations.

If Eustice is in jail he may well be involved in the case now pending which is receiving most local attention. This case involves an action by the owner and operator of the Hampton Restaurant against the county sheriff. These are, more or less, the facts or charges in the case. For a number of years, the Hampton Restaurant has been serving meals to the prisoners in the county jail. The sheriff asked that the county return to an earlier practice of having the meals prepared, under the supervision of the sheriff, in the jail itself, the practice before the county entered into the contract with the Hampton Restaurant. The sheriff asserted that he was having both disciplinary problems and health problems with the prisoners because of the quality of the food being served by the Hampton Restaurant, which, basically, he says, is too greasy.

Following the publication of the charges by the sheriff, the owner of the Hampton Restaurant closed the restaurant to the public charging that the sheriff's public statement had driven off her customers. She is seeking damages, but in the meantime continues to cook for the prisoners, possibly including Eustice, and to deliver food to the jail.

Several persons have rallied to the support of the Hampton, including one county commissioner who said (he has not yet testified under oath) that he has eaten there several times, without notable reaction. When the case came up, I recalled having eaten there once. (I may have eaten there more than once, but I remember only one stop, some five years ago.) Following a rule of mine which is that when eating in restaurants of unknown quality, it is always, or almost always, best to order "the special." I took that evening's special, which was Swiss steak. I remember the gravy.

I do not think I would be a qualified witness in the pending case, however, since my last experience with Swiss steak previous to the encounter at the Hampton, was in a White House lunch with Henry Kissinger, then the National Security Administrator. At that lunch, just Henry and I, I was not asked what I might like to eat; no choices. When the first course came I noted that Henry had a thin consommé; I had cream of celery soup. Then came the main course. Henry had fish, a modest portion. I was given, again without consultation, Swiss steak. No explanation accompanied the offering of the second course. Then came dessert time. "Surely," I thought, "I will be given some choice." It was not to be. Henry had sherbert. I was given a piece of pecan pie. I have had trouble with cream soups, Swiss steaks, and pecan pie ever since.

To understand the complexity of the Hampton case, one should know something about the restaurants of the county. There are not many, but they cover, with some gaps, the full range of service. At one end of the spectrum, is the Inn at "little" Washington, a restaurant of world class, ranking with the best of Paris, of New York, quite possibly better than any restaurant in Washington, D.C. At the center, the "restaurant of the county," with nothing between it and the Inn, is the Corner Post Restaurant, in Flint Hill. This is the restaurant of the local gentry and ladies, the luncheon meeting place of doctors, lawyers, rural mail carriers, retired government employees, colonels, and others. It is the place where Lions Clubs, Rotarians, environmental societies, and others have their banquets.

Then there are, or were, the fringe restaurants, those that come and go, and others of some stability serving local customers but catching customers in transit. Among these was the Hampton Restaurant, invitingly close to Highway 211, enroute to the Skyline Drive, to Old Rag Mountain, and the Luray Caverns. When I first, and last, ate Swiss steak there, there was minor evidence of decline. The sign, which in daytime read RESTAURANT, at night read only AURANT in neon light. The first four letters did not glow, but a restaurant, appearing to be called AURANT, was not uninviting. The name had a kind of French tone. Then the T burned out. And in the dark it was the AURAN, not a bad name for a restaurant. AURAN rings slightly French and personal.

Next the current failed in the RAN section of the sign, and for several years the Hampton was the AU restaurant and so called by the local observers. Then the U went dark. At the time of closing, because of the sheriff's charges, only the A remained, beckoning the hungry traveler in the dark.

This is the most critical case now pending in the county court since it involves property, the county system of justice, gastronomy, and the current interpretation of punishment, which in some advanced prisons has led to the providing of at least five or six different diets; Kosher, sugar-free for diabetics, meat-free and balanced, vegetarian, special foods for Moslems, and, in one case—this one rejected at a Danbury Prison in Connecticut—a demand for sirloin steak and Bristol Creme sherry twice a week, as required by special revelation.

Being forced to eat Hampton Restaurant food, I am sure, will not be ruled as cruel and inhuman treatment. But "Swiss steak" should be banned from all jail and prison menus. The Rappahannock County Jail case may establish a precedent for the nation—unless the widening of Route 211 wipes out the A restaurant and the case.

Miracles on Route 29

Black Birch Becomes Cherry

I MET OVER THE HOLIDAYS a friend who had recently moved from Minnesota to Washington, D.C. He had just gone through his first experience of buying fireplace wood in Georgetown and had found that his experience with wood, its measurement, type, and quality in Minnesota was quite useless in Georgetown.

Having observed the wood trade from both ends of the line—that of a purchaser in Georgetown and, not as a producer, but as an observer of producers in Rappahannock County—I attempted to explain the whole matter to him.

I grew up in a rural community in Minnesota where wood was used for fuel, and I knew from experience, sustained by an education in which measures such as pecks and gills were still taught, that a cord of wood contained 128 cubic feet of wood, allowing for some air spaces, and that the common practice was to measure a cord of wood as four feet by four feet, by eight feet.

My first surprise in buying wood in Georgetown when I moved there, as my friend had, was to discover that though a cord of wood was still four feet high and roughly eight feet in length, in width it was only eighteen inches. I also found that wood was sold as measured in ricks, racks (which in Minnesota were measures of hay) or cribs (which were measures of corn). The measurement actually depended on the dimensions of the pickup truck from which the wood was delivered. The exact volume of wood in a rick, rack, or crib, I never found out. The sellers did allow a prospective buyer to make a quick judgment by eye and then decide whether the price was right.

Being most certain of the quality of oak wood, and of my ability to judge it, I tried to limit my purchases to oak, but sometimes, under duress—either needing the wood or responding to a seller's plea that I buy the last of his load so that he could get back to the county (Culpeper or Rappahannock) before nightfall or before the predicted snowstorm arrived—I did occasionally buy what was described as a "mixed" cord. A "mixed" cord contained, according to the seller, usually some oak, hickory, cherry, locust, possibly ash, maple, and apple. Sometimes my purchase did have the types of woods listed by the seller. Other times it contained woods that did not fit my recollection of their qualities.

On moving to Rappahannock County, I found that hickory, ash, cherry, apple, locust, and other types of trees that grow there are like the same trees in Minnesota, as are the poplar and black birch. However, somewhere and somehow between the wood cutting and the delivery to Georgetown, something happens to some of these woods. Oak, as a rule, I found, which left the country as oak arrived in Georgetown as oak, although its age might have changed along the way. Wood from dead falls sometimes lost age, and green oak took on age, sometimes arriving "cured."

These changes although noteworthy fall short of the miraculous changes to be observed in the case of poplar that leaves the county (either Culpeper or Rappahannock) as poplar but arrives in Georgetown as ash or hickory. Locust, too,

56

enroute sometimes changes into hickory. Black birch is transmuted into cherry and occasionally into apple wood. These miracles, not unlike the scriptural report of the changing of water into wine, seem to occur on Route 29 somewhere between Warrenton and Gainesville, about half the distance between the rural mill and urban Georgetown.

I gave all of this information to the Minnesotan, and then advised him that the character of the wood supplier was also important. For four or five years I had the same provider in Georgetown. I suspected that some kind of territorial or personal imperative had been established in that part of the city for all other wood men seemed to avoid my house. I got the best wood from my supplier in the early years of our association. When later I complained about a cord I had bought, he advised me that one had to make choices among woods, which, he said, were like women. Some gave heat and some gave light. He went on to give me a dissertation on what kind of wood was best for each variety of romantic situation, and as to which of the senses were most affected by different kinds of wood. He recommended oak and hickory for warmth, locust and pine for sound and color, birch and poplar for light, cherry and apple if it were odor you wanted or Romance.

As the years of our relationship ran on, the wood man seemed gradually to lose interest in wood and natural phenomena, and to turn to religion. As he became more religious, the quality of his wood declined. As the last wood bought from him smoldered in my fireplace, I read the card he had left. It encouraged me to have faith in the Lord and in my fellow men (including wood sellers), and advised me to "Keep Smiling."

I advised the Minnesotan, first, to buy only oak and, second, to settle for a "Georgetown Cord" over ricks, racks, cribs and other odd measures and, third, to be careful of philosophical wood sellers and, fourth, to shun those who offered religion, especially with mixed wood.

Picking Presidential Candidates

Rappahannock County Style

OUT OF THE DISCUSSIONS of the presidential campaign of 1988, in country stores, in church yards, in the post offices, and in other places, ten standards—possibly they should be called "commandments"—have emerged as guidelines for picking candidates, and beyond that in choosing a president. It should be noted in fairness that neither candidate of the major parties, Mr. Bush or Mr. Dukakis, scored very well on the Rappahannock scale.

1. The number one standard is that of whether the candidate made his or her announcement of candidacy in February.

If the candidate makes the announcement in February, it can be assumed that the decision was made in that month. If it was not, the candidate should make clear as to when the decision to run was made. Decisions made in February are suspect. So are announcements. February is not looked upon as a good month for thought in Rappahannock County. Even the animals shun decision making in February. It is a time when their life processes, mental and physical are at low ebb. It is a time of deep hibernation. Only the groundhog, by reputation, breaks out on one day, for simple observation and decision, and then returns to hibernation. This suspicion of February has long-standing, historical support. The early Romans dedicated February to the lower world. In that month they worshipped Pluto and the souls of dead ancestors. They looked down and backward. Medieval Christians had a similar attitude towards February. They viewed it as the worst of months. Even a "fair" February was suspect and frowned upon as noted in a Welsh proverb saying:

"A Welshman would rather see his mother dead, than see a fair February."

The New Hampshire vote which used to be taken near mid-March a few days before the spring equinox, is less reliable now that it is held in February.

2. The second standard has to do with the candidate's attitudes toward dogs. A wide variety of breeds is tolerated in Rappahannock County with coon hounds preferred to bird dogs. Dogs generally are well respected in the county and not to be used carelessly or for political purposes. A dog may be used as a witness for the defense of a politican who is in trouble, and, of course, if a candidate's dog is attacked in a political campaign, the candidate not only has the right but the duty to defend the dog. If a candidate includes the family dog or dogs in the program announcing his political plans, he should be discounted. The local informal committee that considered this matter of dogs in politics, was in agreement that Nixon's use of Checkers in his own defense was dog-abuse. Whereas Roosevelt's defense of Fala was commendable.

3. A candidate who frequently quotes the Bible, not only casually, but with the support of chapter and verse, is highly suspect.

4. So is a candidate who represents himself as the sole auditor and frequently quotes, to sustain his positions, politicians who have passed away. A clear cut example cited was that of Larry O'Brien who, as postmaster general at the dedication of a fifteen cent stamp honoring General Marshall, asserted that the General if alive at the time (during the Vietnam War) would have supported the war.

5. Since this county is horse country, and cattle raising is a major industry, and there are cattle shows, and horse shows and races, any presidential candidate who promises that he or she will pick a blue ribbon cabinet rather than, say, a red ribbon one or a green ribbon cabinet, is suspected of either exaggerating or of lacking in understanding of how difficult it is to pick a blue ribbon winner.

6. This is also Thomas Jefferson country, the Jeffersonian concept of the vice-presidency is strongly endorsed. Jefferson saw that office as a good one, one which gave him time in the winter to meditate on philosophy, and in the summer to study nature. There was no attempt on his part to give "new meaning" to the office. A presidential candidate who promises to give new meaning to the office should be questioned closely, as should a vice-presidential candidate who participates in any such project. What was good enough for Jefferson should be good enough for any vice-president, especially since during his term in that office Jefferson did not waste time trying to give new meaning to the office but spent it constructively inventing, among other things, a leather buggy top and an improved plough.

7. Physical fitness, especially that manifest in strength gained from work, is well regarded in the county, but jogging is regarded as a little strange. Presidential candidates who are given to jogging and to bragging about their time and distance achievements, especially since such efforts may leave them a little short of oxygen going to the brain, are rated low on the candidate scale.

8. A knowledge of the significance of prime numbers by a presidential candidate is considered desirable. The principal advocate of this qualification is Lyt Woods, formerly the County Forester. Lyt explains the importance of such numbers relative to the life cycle of the 13- and the 17-year

locusts, noting that the eggs of locusts with a life cycle measurable in prime numbers, are not likely to hatch in the same year in which their natural predators are present in force. Thus he notes that the 13-year locust might avoid potential enemies that had a two-year life cycle, since those enemies, if the cycles were properly adjusted, would appear in the 12th or 14th years, thus missing the 13th. Enemies with a three-year cycle would appear in the 12th and 15th years; those with a four-year cycle, in the 12th and 16th; those with a five-year cycle, in the 10th and 15th, etc., thus giving the locust a good chance of surviving in numbers. The relevance of this to politics is that a president who understands prime numbers should seek to arrange his election, or his dealing with controversial issues, in such a way that his natural political enemies, principally the House of Representatives and the Senate, might not be present or, if present, in a weakened condition. Thus a single seven-year presidential term might be better than the two four-year terms now allowed.

9. Since reading economic signs and predicting changes in economic conditions is an important presidential responsibility, the indicators and measures used in making such studies and determinations are important. Presidential candidates should be checked to see whether, in addition to the usual measures used by economists, business analysts, bankers, and other experts—such as gross national products, credit, money supply, corporate profits, housing starts, etc.—indicators of special significance in Rappahannock County are also included.

There are two such local standards of special relevance. Actually one of these standards is more evident in Franklin County in southwestern Virginia, but it has some bearing on the economy of Rappahannock County. Over the years economic observers have noted that the production of illegal whiskey, i.e., moonshine, and the number of operating stills, discovered and destroyed by revenue agents, reflect quite immediately changes in general economic conditions, in taxation, and in some more limited and immediate economic operations. Thus a rise in taxes on liquor, in Virginia or in adjoining states, is likely to stimulate an increase in moonshining. A fall in corn prices, or a more general economic depression, is also likely to spur production, whereas a rise in corn prices, or an increase in sugar prices such as that which followed the embargo of Cuban sugar in 1961, will decrease liquor production in Franklin and Rappahannock County.

A second significant indicator, signaling both long term and short term economic trends in the County is, according to country storekeepers, the change in the sales of blueberry muffin mix. In periods of rising optimism and expectations, and prosperity, blueberry muffin sales are high. A downturn in the economy is indicated by generally falling sales of blueberry muffin mixes. According to these same storekeepers, oatmeal sales are useless as an indicator and remain relatively constant throughout the whole cycle of business and economic change. During recession, it appears, the poor eat less and therefore buy less oatmeal; but those losses are offset by increased purchases of oatmeal by persons whose income is declining and who therefore are cutting down on blueberry muffin mix purchases.

10. The last test, possibly the most important, in Rappahannock County is difficult to apply. Basically it raises the question of whether the candidates know that pigs and cattle have to be handled differently. If one is attempting to drive cows, he or she must start them slowly, sing to them, and gradually speed up the drive to stampede level, as one gets them near where one wants them. (The House of Representatives is best handled by this method.) It was the favorite, almost the only method, used by President Johnson. Pigs, on the other hand, must be started into action under near panic

conditions through shouting at them, preferably in Latin (*Sui, Sui*), beating on the pig troughs and fences, giving them no time to think. They can be allowed to slow down gradually so that they arrive at the appointed place at a slow walk, believing that they have made choices all along the way. Pig techniques are preferred and are most effective in moving the Senate to action. A candidate should also know that in very cold weather a pig will do almost anything to keep its nose warm. The remains of five prehistoric pigs were once discovered in a glacier frozen to death in a circle.

Rural Mail Box

Endangered?

FIVE YEARS AGO I noted what I thought was a threat to the Rural Mail Box. I feared that it had become an endangered species, not as birds or beasts, or fish or flowers, or weeds, or trees, are threatened by blight or mold, or spreading suburbs and freeways, or industrial growth or new dams or waterways, as in the case of the louse wort and the snail darter, but by the Insurance Institute of Highway Safety.

The Insurance Institute had discovered that under some conditions the roadside Rural Free Delivery mail boxes, together with their sustaining posts, supports, and mountings, were a threat to the life and limb of some automobile drivers and passengers, and might do damage to the automobile itself, to say nothing of the insurance companies.

On the basis of limited study and what it called "sketchy data," the Institute published a "Status Report" charging that mail boxes were a serious roadside hazard. The report was taken up by the United States Postal Service, which, stirred by the results of the Texas study and by the report of the Insurance Institute, announced that it was "looking into the whole matter" in order "to explore the possibility of establishing safety requirements for mail box supports," an example of how some of the things done by government are begun by non-governmental institutions, by private businesses, and especially by the institutes supported by private businesses.

The Insurance Institute announced that it would continue to sponsor research in the hope of developing safe mail boxes and safe mountings.

I anticipated that a soft plastic mail box like those given to country newspaper subscribers by publishers, a new design, certainly, without the classical lines of the standard U.S. mail box available at hardware stores and from mail order houses, in basic unpainted galvanized gray, or painted black would be required. I expected that standard specifications as to placement, height of standards, composition and shape of supporting structures, a new color, scientifically tested so as not to attract the attention of any automobile drivers, might be forthcoming.

I expected that cedar posts commonly used as supports for mail boxes in wetlands would have to go, as well as solid oak in temperate zones on reasonably high ground. The trusted locust, the only sure post in termite and dry rot zones, would be banned and cantilevered mountings declared illegal.

At the time, the Postal Service spokesman said, "I don't think anyone knows how large the problem might be."

I feared the worst, but now five years after the early studies there is no evidence that the Postal Department has made any moves. The problem may have been greater than those who instituted and pursued the study anticipated. Counter studies may have shown how many lives were saved because rural mail boxes of various shapes and colors, on a variety of mountings along the road, have kept sleepy drivers awake, have warned persons driving in a fog of either mist or alcohol of where the road ended and where the ditch began, or have marked in snow blown plains the line between road and field, and of how drivers alerted and forewarned by hitting mail boxes have been saved from the worse fate of running into ditches, or hitting trees, or rocky banks.

In any case I note that the standard box still survives, and that personal tastes, and creativity, are still allowed in choice of boxes and in placement and in mountings. In this county "Uncle Sams," cut out of board or plank, offer boxes to the mail man or woman. Old walking ploughs, set in cement with boxes mounted at the beam's end, are in evidence, as are boxes held between wheels, salvaged from hay rakes and cultivators. The welded chain support, sure to draw attention, has some adherents. Boxes mounted on pipes set in milk cans filled with cement, which can be set up again when knocked down by cars or snow ploughs, survive, as do boxes painted in any but the "official colors," and miniatures of house, or barn, and even of country churches. The locust post remains the dominant support, at least in Rappahannock County.

Mainstreet Porch

Consumers Dis-Union

Divided We Stand

CONSUMER PROTECTION is not given a very high priority among the matters of concern to the residents of Rappahannock County. Major purchases such as used cars, land, houses, horses, and cattle are usually based on the buyer's knowledge of what he or she is buying or on trust in the seller, with little or no help from organizations like Consumers Union. Consequently the recent publication of that organization's 50-year retrospective, entitled *I'll Buy That*, did not stir much response in the county—especially since the 50 "small wonders and big deals" which the editors of the publication said had revolutionized the lives of consumers had at best a marginal effect on the lives of consumers in Rappahannock County.

Of the 50 items emphasized in the book, ten involve automobiles, including the introduction of the seat belt. There is no evidence as to what effect the belt has had on life in the county, but of the other nine, including such innovations as the automatic transmission, only one, the jeep, or four-wheel drive vehicle, has had any noticeable effect on the way of life in the county.

The effects of enriched bread, tampons, Dr. Spock's baby book, disposable diapers, the pill, and fluoridized water, all considered by Consumers Union to have significant national impact, have not had measurable impact in the county. Nor have various sound and picture recording, reproducing, and transmitting devices, such as T.V., compact discs, hi fi's, LP records, transistors, magnetic tapes, VCRs or satellite dishes, although most are in evidence and in use in the county.

Detergents have replaced homemade soap, a scarcely revolutionary change. Air travel in and out of the county is limited to what may be handled by one grass landing strip. Suburbia has not yet reached the county. There is no McDonald's, no supermarket, and no real shopping mall. Credit cards, excepting for purchase of gasoline, are not widely in use. Checks for all purposes are commonly made out to "cash."

Power lawn mowers, according to Consumers Union, have had a significant effect on suburban development and suburban living. This phenomenon has encouraged larger lawns, thus providing exercise for suburbanites, practically destroying Sunday as a day of rest, and leading to the formulation of great principles of community living such as "Never trust a neighbor who offers to cut your lawn or trim your side of a hedge." Lawns may be slightly larger and better kept with the grass cut shorter than it was when cut by hay mowers or bush hogs, but power mowers have had at most a marginal effect in the county.

More significant than the new products and institutions which have had little or no effect in the county are those which have been resisted, for good reasons and with social and community benefits. Among these are three of special note: air-conditioning, the electric dryer, and running shoes.

Air conditioning, according to product analysts, and societal psychologists, has eliminated the differences between the sun belt and the snow belt. Also eliminated, or in the process of being eliminated, are both open and screened porches, front and back, thus doing away with a traditional courting place with minimal family supervision and leaving only the automobile as the place for this important social rite.

Rappahannock County is not in the snow belt or in the sun belt. It is in what might best be called the "sleet belt." Air-conditioning has not caught on here. Nor has the porch, which has been a part of houses in this area, been eliminated. Both screened porches and open porches are common on old houses and on newly built ones, both front and back, and sometimes on three sides with a deck added on the fourth for good measure. More substantial older houses not only had porches at ground level, but also on the second story.

Porches in Rappahannock are not limited in use to one or two functions. They serve multiple purposes, the standard one of shade and protection from rain; the social one of sitting and talking and watching; an additional one of providing storage space for washing machines and other household equipment and utensils; for wood storage during the winter; for display of flowers, especially hanging pots of geraniums; also for pottery, ceramic and pressed concrete animals and birds; with open space beneath the porch floor used for more storage, plus home or haven for dogs and cats.

The electric washer and dryer, in the opinion of Consumers Union, have had significant national effect. The washer has been accepted and is widely used in the county, but it functions in a way little different from the earlier hand-washing machines. The dryer has had no such acceptance. Clothes of many shapes, colors, and uses still hang on backyard clothes lines on Monday and Tuesday, the traditional days for drying clothes. Drying is done by sun and wind, and the social good of talk across backyard fences is preserved.

Running shoes (once called tennis shoes) have made a revolutionary mark in backward countries where they have become standard footwear, and also among women in more advanced societies. Once the shoes of "little old ladies in tennis shoes," they have been taken over by emancipated professional and paraprofessional women (at least on the way to work and on the way home) as a mark of independence from the hobbling custom imposed by high-heeled shoes. The use of running shoes has brought on the manufacture and marketing of at least one new product, now advertised on television, designed to neutralize the odor of walking or running shoes at home, in carrying bags, or in office file cabinets. "Odor Eater," one such product, is a far cry from the reality of twenty-five years ago when in late summer, a boy's "Keds" became so rank that mothers ordered them put out of doors at night along with the cat. Running shoes have made some inroads in Rappahannock County especially in their use by women, but the basic and dominating footwear is still the calf-length, unlined, snake proof, leather Rappahannock County boot.

Consumers Union should not be too disappointed in the failure of Rappahannock County residents to conform to the Union's findings, keeping in mind that the produce buyer in Sperryville buys Genseng, and live rattle snakes.

Where Old Cars Go

Rappahannock Retirement

THERE IS A DRIVE ON in Rappahannock County to rid the county of old, junked, and abandoned cars. The project is state supported and promoted. Basically, it provides for a payment of fifty dollars per car that is collected. The formula for distributing the fifty dollars is flexible. Ten dollars goes to the county. This provision could be a source of considerable revenue for the county, as the number of visible cars, or parts of cars, in various stages of neglect or abandonment is considerable. If it is assumed that the cars not visible from the road outnumber those within range of vision by seven to one, as the estimated ratio of ice not seen is to that which is visible in iceberg sighting, old cars and hulks could for several years be a major crop in the county. Yet the response to the new program has been limited.

Rappahannock County does not give up its houses, its machinery, its customs easily.

Many houses still in use are over two hundred years old. Some parts of houses, especially chimneys, are of like age. Houses once abandoned, as a rule, are not torn down, at least by older residents. They are left, on the possibility that they may be used again, and if that re-use is not likely, as a reminder to those who survive of the passage, by death or abandonment, of the last residents in the houses. Chimneys are left standing long after all vestiges of houses they once served have disappeared.

The site of old mills is marked by crumbling walls, evidence of dams and of mill ponds and mill races. Mills of later vintage, many of them, still stand, some converted into houses, some into antique and craft shops, some just waiting. Silos stand alone in fields and farm yards, the barns they complemented fallen into decay, or torn down and moved. Some churches have survived loss of faith or of faithful; a few are changed to houses or to shops, and some stand in window-boarded vigil over grass-grown cemeteries. Old filling stations and banks closed during the depression remain, reborn to new purposes and life as antique stores.

Old farm machinery stands in farm yards or in meadows; the most prominent and most numerous among them, the first significant aid to hay makers, the horse-drawn dump rake. Abandoned, or kept in reserve, on suspicion that newer rakes and bailers may break down, the old rakes seem to attract a protective growth of burning nettles.

But the automobile outmatches all other things, houses, churches, machinery, in survivability. The poet Philip Booth, in a poem entitled "Maine," has declared that "when old cars get retired they go to Maine." He then describes them, some as being like cows grazing quietly behind old barns. Others sit in place with backends jacked up, the wheels replaced by pulley or circular saw to grind feed or cut wood. Engine blocks from some are dropped in the Atlantic to serve as anchors for buoys and boats at rest.

Not all old cars go to Maine. Many go to Rappahannock. What few new cars come here may well stay until dismantled or abandoned. Most cars start life in the county as used cars, bought new first in other places. There is no new car sales outlet in the county. There are used car sales lots, and lots with dismantled cars and parts for sale, as well as the scattered remains, the object of the state and county search and solicitation. Some, the still favored ones on blocks, stand in sheds and barns. Some, abandoned when houses were abandoned, crouch in growths of brambles, or in locust thickets. Others hide under cover of honeysuckle or kudzu. Engines under repair, or despaired of, hang from tripods or branches of oak or maple, draining or drained, like deer hung out to cure or butchered hogs, to cool.

It is anticipated that the state and county project may well fall short of the measure of success hoped for by those who conceived it.

Windchill in the County

Keep Your Clothes On

A PROPOSAL TO SELL THE U.S. WEATHER BUREAU, announced near the beginning of the Reagan administration, seems to have been lost forever. Possibly no private companies, or practitioners of weather predictions, such as Willard Scott nationally or Bob Ryan locally, fearing malpractice suits, made any offers to buy. Insurance charges may have been too high.

In any event the reasons given for the proposed sale were never very clear. If reducing the national debt had been the objective, it would have been better to offer for sale more profitable properties, such as radio and television licenses. The right to graze on the public "mind" and "will" could have been granted to the highest bidder in somewhat the same way that the rights to graze sheep and cattle on public lands are distributed.

Although the administration spokesperson, who made the announcement of the proposed sale, did not say so, it was generally assumed that the administration thought that the private sector could give us better weather or more of it, for less money; that weather analysis and predicting might become more competitive and consequently, according to the general belief of the administration that the private sector can always do better than the public one, we might not only get better weather but more accurate predictions as well.

The whole matter received little serious or prolonged consideration at the country store. Predicting the weather in Rappahannock County has long been suspect.

Rappahannock County usually gets more rain and snow than is predicted for the general area. Wind forces, however, are moderated by the protection given by the Blue Ridge Mountains. The county is usually neither as hot nor as cold as its adjacent counties, or weather centers. Because of the uncertainties, persons living

73

here have come to rely on local students of weather, both for long term predictions and for short term ones. Some experts use old German and Swiss forecasting devices, in which the approach of bad weather is indicated by the appearance at the door of the weather house of a scolding woman armed with a broom, and approach of continuing good weather, by a jovial, satisfied man. Protest against this evidence of sexual discrimination has been limited, and may well remain so, if the local weather forecasts maintain a minimal level of superiority over those made more scientifically, or by a balanced crew of male and female predictors.

County weather experts have also held out against the Centigrade measure of temperature. They have stuck with Fahrenheit.

Predictions of rainfall here are made in simple measurements of inches, or parts of an inch. No one gives any attention to 20 percent chance of rain, or any such relative measurements. Heavy snow, here, is distinguished from light snow on the basis of moisture content. The measure of depth of snow is estimated in inches. Windchill reports are not taken seriously, since few persons will take the time to apply the formula, which requires one to take off his or her clothes, then take the wind velocity and multiply it by one and a half, and then subtract this figure from the temperature, if the temperature is above zero, and add it if the temperature is below zero (or both add and subtract if the process carries one's calculations past the zero point).

The discomfort index, a mathematical combination of temperature and humidity readings applicable to government employees in Washington working in non-air-conditioned buildings and triggering their early release, is not recognized in the county.

Generally the forecasts of local weather are tested against the *Farmer's Almanac* as the best source of weather information for Rappahannock County.

Trash

Route 618 Subject to Scientific Study

IN RECENT YEARS the three-mile stretch of Route 618, from the site of the old Land's Mill to the Hazel River was possibly the best kept, litter-free stretch of road in Virginia. This was not due to the thoroughness of the highway department, but almost exclusively, because of the care and attention given to the road and roadside by Hoppy Hopkins, a retired or semi-retired professor, and his wife Jane.

Following Hoppy's death both the litter along the road and the increase in the groundhog population in the area testify to his absence, for along with his concern over litter, Hoppy was an unrelenting groundhog hunter.

I and others who live along the road have taken note of the slowly accumulating litter, and out of concern for the beauty of the road, and because of guilt over having neglected a duty which we had come to leave to Hoppy and to his wife Jane, we even began to talk about doing something about the situation. First we postponed our undertaking until summertime, waiting, we said, for the honeysuckle to recede and then for the poison ivy to die.

Meanwhile I conducted an objective, socio-psychological survey of the litter along the way, in the manner in which I thought Hoppy would have wanted us to study the matter.

First, I noted that the traffic on the road was a controlled factor. Traffic is relatively light, the vehicles generally driven by persons who know where they are and where they are going. Occasionally a lost driver may get on the road, but as a rule there are few transient motorists. The vehicles I noted seem to be about standard mix, except for a more than average percentage of pickup trucks, during the hunting season.

In our first study, I acknowledged that we did not have comparative figures, and therefore could not discover or report trends. I recognized also that some of the litter items undoubtedly are still concealed by honeysuckle, poison ivy, ferns, and other plant growth, and that later figures, adjusted, will be more accurate.

I submit my findings as within the range of about a four percent margin of error, which seems to be the standard for error in television network political projections.

I found as my first significant observation that there was a full range of drink container litter from one brandy bottle to one milk carton. The heaviest concentrations, or highest numbers of litter items, were beer bottles and cans and similar containers for sugar loaded drinks.

By a clear margin, the major litterer was the Budweiser beer drinker, casting both bottles and cans at the roadside. Not only did the Bud containers outnumber any other single brand of cast-off containers, but they outnumbered all other beers put together, including Michelob, Old Milwaukee, Pilsner, Red White and Blue, and Schlitz, Pabst, and single entries of Coors, and a beer called Goebel. Budweiser might well add a line to its commercial, urging its drinkers not to litter, in their happiness.

Among the soft drink cans counted along the road, the difference was not quite as marked as it is among beer cans. Mountain Dew led all the rest by a considerable margin, that is one on one, but not in overall totals. Pepsi Cola and Coca Cola ranked in a tie for second, followed by Dr. Pepper, Seven Up, and then Tab and Diet Pepsi, and one abandoned container that once held some kind of grape drink. The significant conclusion from this data is that Mountain Dew drinkers are different, and that those who drink sugared drinks seem more ready to litter than those who are into diet drinks.

The data on solid food litter and containers for non-liquids was more difficult to gather. Zagnut candy wrappers and bags that once held cheese popcorn, along with plastic cups, were most numerous. In statistically insignificant numbers I noted also several potato chip bags, a cup-cake mold, and one Milky Way (the candy of the Olympics) wrapper.

According to my estimates, if the standard $50 littering fine could have been assessed for each violation in this three-mile stretch of road, the state could have collected some $5,000!

Listening

Rand Corporation Method

THE RAND CORPORATION, one of America's leading corporations, which also features a think tank, has for some time been running an advertisement in the better business magazines touting a course in "Listening." The advertisement suggests, if it does not positively assert, that most persons, or many, fail to rise in the business world and in the professions because they do not listen, or do not listen correctly.

I did not subscribe to Rand Corporation's course, but was moved by its advertisements to wonder whether I was listening well. Possibly, I thought, I had been missing something or many things. Possibly I was not thinking clearly because I had not been listening.

I resolved to listen attentively for a whole day, beginning just before dawn when I listened to the varied notes of the small birds, wood sparrows, principally, I think, in the cedar hedge adjacent to my bedroom window. After a half hour of this listening, I heard the first morning cawing of the crows, followed by the cry of the catbirds, and of the blue jays, and then the drumming of woodpeckers on dead pine and tulip trees. By seven o'clock, when I should have been getting up to begin work on a book I am supposed to be writing, I was still in bed, listening.

New sounds had come on, domestic ones: the crowing of Mary McCoy's rooster and the bleating of her goats. The early morning plaintive mooing of Bill Senkewitz's cow, either calling for a calf, or for a neighbor's bull. Then came the raucous sound of Nelson Lane's jackass, reminding me of dawn in Jerusalem, and prompting me to listen in vain for the cry of muezzin, calling the faithful to morning prayer.

All through the day, I kept listening, according to the prescription of Rand Corporation. Each time, as I was about to stop listening and go in to my typewriter, another sound distracted me: the mid-morning scream of a hawk, the skittering sound of the kingfisher as he skimmed above the pond water, the September hummingbird, buzzing in late flowers, the noon-day yelp of wild turkeys. I did interrupt my listening for lunch, but still unsatisfied and apprehensive that, if I left off my listening, I might spoil the whole Rand Corporation scheme.

I returned to listening in the afternoon resting in a lawn chair. I noted the changing sound of the wind as it first came over the mountain, moving the high pines and oaks and tulip trees that marked the ridge, and then worked down to gentler leaves of hickory and ash and to the almost soundless movement of the birch leaves and of the weeping willows. When no wind blew, I could hear the maple leaves ticking onto the ground, counting off the end of summer.

During my afternoon walk, I continued to listen, to the sound of squirrels and chipmunks among the leaves and of rabbits, to the grunting to John Glasker's pig loose in the woods, unless it was the resident bear I heard. I noted the changing sound of Beaver Dam Creek as more water fed into it on its run down to the old mill site. I noted also, in Thoreau fashion, the sound of the jets overhead, and of trucks on distant Route 552, as well as a muffled rumble of thunder beyond the mountains.

Late afternoon brought on the bobwhite and the mockingbirds, and at dusk the sad singing of coon hounds waiting for night. Then, as darkness settled in, the bass notes of the bullfrogs followed and the shrill scrapings of the cicadas, the hooting of the owls, again the lonely bellowing of cattle and the jackass once more.

I had listened all day, and had come to none of the clear insights and understandings Rand Corporation had all but promised. Nor had I touched pen or typewriter.

An Endangered Species?

Cold Comfort

Building Character in the Country

A BIOGRAPHICAL SKETCH I once read of Archbishop Weakland of Milwaukee made a special point of the fact that the Archbishop, as a small boy, lived in a house in which the bedrooms were unheated, and that on cold mornings he would go downstairs in his night clothes to change in the heat that radiated from a central coal stove. This experience, among others, had, according to the article, formed the Archbishop's positive character. The report reminded me that I had had the same experience, in the same kind of house, but I had been unaware of its character-building potential. I recall that it was rather pleasant, even exciting, to change clothes, close to the coal stove in the living room, watching the flames through the stove's isinglass windows, a pleasure which was lost when what we called "city water" was put in the town and a furnace and hot water heating system installed in our family house. The new heating arrangement was called "central heating," a misnomer, I think, since it was not central heat but distributed heat with radiators in every room. The old system, if it can be called a system, was truly central, and not much more than that. In any case, central or not, I was exposed to the character building of the cold bedroom and the hot stove during my formative years, and may have, without my knowing it, benefitted from the experience.

The report of the Archbishop's hardship and character building moved me to recall other reports of character-building experiences which may have affected my character. For example, in the presidential campaign of 1972 it was noted that Senator Muskie, one of the candidates, had as a boy taken Saturday night baths in a wash tub set on the kitchen floor. This information was not presented as incidental information but as having bearing on Mr. Muskie's presidential qualifications. I had had the same treatment but had never associated anything in my character with that fact. My brother and I had bathed in the same way, again before we got the city water and the furnace and a bathroom complete with tub. The water we used was cistern water, moderately warm as it came from the reservoir on the cook stove, with an extra shot of boiling water from the tea kettle added. As I remember we enjoyed the baths, more than later ones in proper bathtubs. We were repeatedly warned against splashing water on the kitchen floor. This restraint may have been character building.

Then in 1975, I discovered that I had either missed a chance to build my character or that my character had been built in some measure without my knowing of it. In that year *Newsweek* magazine, in a full page advertisement, set out what they considered both the negative and the positive attributes of Jimmy Carter as a potential president of the United States. Among the positive ones was listed the fact that Jimmy as a boy had used, down in Georgia, an outdoor toilet. I had that same experience but had never thought to take any public credit for it. In fact I had had the experience under conditions more taxing and demanding than the conditions in Georgia. In Minnesota there was the summer exposure to bumblebees and outhouse wasps, which I assume was also the case in Georgia. But the winter exposure in Minnesota, in twenty-below-zero weather, must have been an even stronger force for developing courage and fortitude than any exposure in Georgia.

I might add a fourth and possibly more powerful character-building experience than those of the Archbishop's, Senator Muskie's, and Jimmy Carter's. My test is cleaning out a chicken house after the first spring thaw, following a long, frozen winter.

Many residents of Rappahannock County have had their characters formed through such tests and trials. Some still are being tried, tested, and proved.

Promise of Springtime
Optimism from Jehovah's Witness

AFTER AN ABSENCE of nearly two weeks I returned to Rappahannock County on a Friday early in May. I was apprehensive that I might well have missed the best part of May. I found that I had missed some things. The apple blossoms evidently had come and gone while I was absent, for the apple trees were now in green leaf. There was no sign of redbud at wood's edge, or of wild cherry. The dogwood was still in bloom, however. Golden ragweed was thick in the pastures, and so were the buttercups.

I found the wild azaleas blooming where they should have been, along Route 618. The grass in the pasture was as high as the knees of the cows, and the hay in the meadow was ready for cutting. Goat's-beard and wild phlox, and sweet cicely and poppies bloomed at roadside. A few May apple blossoms still clung to the stems beneath the umbrella leaves. So, encouraged, I bought tomato plants at Burke's store when I went to the post office on Saturday morning to pick up my mail.

On returning home I decided to check through the mail before planting the tomatoes. I was in for a shock. There was no spring-like optimism, not even hope, in my mail. Evidently the prophets of gloom, the managers of direct mail programs, know not how the seasons run.

First I opened a letter from *The American Sentinel*, warning me that American children are being brainwashed and that unless the process is stopped, and our nuclear arms build-up continued, we and the children may eventually be destroyed by Soviet nuclear arms. Offsetting this letter was another, from the Community for Creative Non-Violence, suggesting that the only way we can escape nuclear destruction is to stop building nuclear arms.

I received an appeal, endorsed by Katherine Hepburn, asking for support for population control, in some form or other, and restating the Malthusian theory that the world would be destroyed by excessive numbers of people. Countering this appeal was one from The Right to Life organization, asserting that population control, in some forms, would destroy civilization. The choices were not easy.

There was a letter from a Republican Committee asking for help in electing a Republican president and making predictions of dire things to come if a Republican were not chosen. Discounting or offsetting that letter was one from the Democratic National Committee informing me that the chairman of that party thinks I will agree with him that the election of a Republican president might well be disastrous for the nation.

There was an appeal, over the signature of James Watt, the former Secretary of the Interior, asking for help and saying that President Reagan had been a voice "in the wilderness." Critics of the President, I recalled, had been charging that Reagan wanted to destroy the wilderness. Why, I wondered, was he "crying" there. The Secretary, in any case, in biblical spirit, wanted help in subduing the wilderness. His appeal was balanced, or countered, by a letter from the *National Geographic Magazine*, urging me to buy a book entitled *Our Threatened Inheritance*, so that I would know what that inheritance is, how it is threatened, and what to do about the threat. There seemed no middle ground, or wilderness.

There was an appeal from the American Heart Association asking for contributions in support of research in heart disease, a good cause. There was no clear counter appeal to this, or to appeals for help in cancer care and study. There was instead a distracting lead article, in a pamphlet called "Executive Health," "On That Treacherous Gland, Your Prostate."

I was becoming depressed, near despair. There seemed no way out, all escapes were blocked.

I decided that I had had all of the warnings and admonitions I could stand, and was about to throw the rest of my mail, unopened, into the waste basket, when I was distracted by the barking of my dog. When I went out to investigate, I found that a large, green Cadillac, of some years' service, had been driven into my driveway. I thought that it might be a bottle gas salesman, or possibly someone intent on selling me a Culligan water-softener system. It was neither. It was a Jehovah's Witness, who had come over the mountain from Luray, in Page County, Virginia, to warn the people of Rappahannock County of the signs and portents of the destruction of the world and the coming of the Kingdom.

I listened to his message, to his quotations from the Bible, the promise of Armageddon, with rising optimism. I told him that after the depressing mail I had just been reading, that his words had uplifted my spirit. I bought three pamphlets from him and after he had gone, planted my tomatoes in trust that I might get one more crop before the end.

Uncle's Day

A Force for Family Stability

A *NEW YORK TIMES* article once proposed the establishment of a national "Aunt's Day" to go along with, or supplement, Mother's Day and Father's Day, and also Grandparents' Day. The *Times*'s article made no reference to the latter day, which has been in existence since 1978, when the Congress of the United States, despite its concern over difficult problems of that time, such as energy, inflation, taxes, and "detente," found time to be thoughtful and considerate. The Congress passed a resolution setting up "Grandparents' Day" and set the first Sunday after Labor Day as the date for its observance.

The report on the resolution required, by the rules of the House of Representatives, an inflationary impact statement. At the time of the passage of the resolution it was predicted that establishing the special day would have no such impact. The experience of the years since the passage of the resolution seems to bear out the prediction. There is no objective evidence that the establishment of the special day has had much effect on family relationships, stability, general happiness, or on the economy.

Now Aunt's Day is proposed. I have no particular objection to such an establishment. Aunts have been and still are important in the family structure, but their role remains, certainly in Rappahannock County, what it always has been, primarily supportive, generally of mothers, sometimes of fathers, also of grandparents.

It is the role of the uncle in family functioning that needs attention, revival, and recognition according to the collective judgment of resident uncles in the county. Establishing a "National Uncle's Day," might do much to accomplish this objective.

The decline of the family in America, according to recent, unpublished studies of limited scope in Rappahannock County, is directly traceable to the de-emphasis and discounting of the role of uncles. The uncle was not supportive of parents as were aunts. Uncles were a free force. They were a place of refuge from dominating aunts (for small boys especially). Uncles were not exactly subversive of parental authority, but they were at least a refuge, a source of contrary position and of a second opinion. They were a bridge between family and society, a role not fulfilled by the traditional aunt. Uncles were useful for transmitting the facts of life, when prudish parents hesitated and the birds and bees were not understood. When the uncle prevailed, unrestrained youths were few.

The term "Dutch Uncle," a stern advisor, roughly comparable to the "Irish Aunt," has made its way into the language. But this conception of the uncle's role is at best a limited and inadequate one. Uncles should be stern about one-fourth of the time and understanding and encouraging the other three-fourths of the time. According to Patrick O'Connor,

> "All children should be Japanese.
> All women (mothers and wives) Italian.
> All grandparents, Jewish.
> All men (husbands and fathers,) Montenegrin.
> All aunts, single, (German, I would say)
> And all uncles, Irish."

The essence of unclehood has been best expressed by Margaret Atwood in a poem called "Game After Supper," from which the following is taken:

> "I am hiding in the long grass
> with my two. . .cousins.

We hear crickets and our own hearts,
close to our ears,
though we giggle, we are afraid.

From the shadows around
the corner of the house
a tall man is coming to find us.

He will be an uncle
if we are lucky."

All of which, as agreed among the sages of the county, adds up to a good case for a "National Uncle's Day."

Under Siege

A Single Man's House

A MAN'S HOUSE, that is, the house of a man living alone, may be his castle, but if he is not on guard, it will not long be his home. The house of a bachelor is almost always under attack, by persons, men and women, acting as men and women always do, according to Aristotle, under some aspect of good.

The attack on the home may come from strangers, or near strangers, or casual visitors, but more often it comes from close friends and from relatives. It may come from males, but more often, according to current cultural attitudes, it will come from women, sisters and daughters especially.

Any and all of these types of persons are prone to make suggestions about a man's home, how it should be decorated, furnished, how it should be run. They may even do things to it, with or without his approval, sometimes when he is watching, sometimes when he is not watching—things they would never think of suggesting or doing to a woman's domicile.

The potential aggressors are no respectors of wealth, or of rank, or of standard of living. They are as likely to direct attacks on a Fifth Avenue apartment, decorated and furnished in the highest and most expensive style, as on the most modest of male living quarters.

The first challenge is usually negative, restrained, and subtle. Sometimes it is preceded or accompanied by an apology. At the higher and more sophisticated levels of existence, it may be no more than an offhand mention of a decorator who would "certainly be challenged" by the architecture of the building, by its internal lighting or its exposure."

In cruder forms, at more common and more modest levels of existence, intervention may come in reference to condition of slipcovers or curtains or, without words, a not-so-surreptitious running of a finger along a windowsill, across a tabletop, a picture frame, or a lamp. This action may be followed by a questioning announcement that one's cleaning person needs another day of work each week.

These negative attacks can usually be ignored without lasting harm to friendship or to family or personal relationships. In some cases they can be accepted, acceded to, without yielding or sacrificing the integrity of one's home.

It is from the positive frontal attacks that the serious threats arise. This aggression against a man's home often begins in seemingly harmless suggestions that new curtains would brighten a room, and an apparent unselfish offer to help in the selection or even to make the selection. The breakthrough, or break-in, may come with a gift of a throw rug or a pillow or two, followed by the suggestion that the room colors do not match the rug or pillow. The lamps in a man's house, too, are easy and early targets of the remodelers or refurnishers. The lamps are especially vulnerable to attack if they are made out of old shell casings, fire-extinguisher tanks, baseball bats, used wine bottles, or old cornets.

A man's kitchen is especially vulnerable and attractive as a target for women visitors, many of whom seem to assume that, despite women's liberation of labor and of responsibility, the kitchen in a single man's home is partly, at least, in their jurisdiction.

The intrusive action may take the form of an open takeover of cooking or other food preparation. In its less immediate and aggressive form the intrusion is likely to show in the rearrangement of kitchen cupboards. (Daughters, according to my observations, are most likely to take this action.) After the rearrangers have been given the run of a kitchen for any length of time, the man of the home is likely to find on going to the cupboard, in trusting Mother Hubbard manner, not a bare cupboard but one changed, changed utterly. He is likely to find dishes where he once kept cooking supplies; cooking supplies where once glasses stood, etc. Cooking utensils are likely to have been moved according to some mysterious logic I do not understand: pot covers gone from the drawer under the stove—a place that seems a perfectly satisfactory repository—to the oven; frying pans removed from the oven and concealed in some secret place. One may find his refrigerator cleaned—rather, cleaned out. Good food that he had been saving for a week or two gone. And then there is the special case of vanilla extract. I have three daughters. Each, I have found, has a different preference for the placement of that cooking aid.

Bathrooms, next to kitchen, are in line of the reformers' fire. Sometimes the interventions are marginally acceptable, as when, for example, they take the form of gifts of matching towels, or a new shower curtain replacing one that was still good but hanging by only three or four clamps. . . . More often the intervention borders on the irresponsible and the insulting, as in the casting away of good soap remnants, or in the obvious, evidence-leaving act of cleaned mirrors, sinks, and medicine cabinets.

The ultimate challenge, possibly confrontation, begins with the suggestion that pictures should be moved, raised or lowered, regrouped, or hung in some other room, possibly to be taken down altogether, given to a church bazaar or to the volunteer firemen's sale, or even thrown away. This move may have been preceded by a gift of picture or pictures or may be followed by such a gift, which the householder, or homeholder, must either put on his walls, or terminate a friendship or relationship of some other order, or live under continuing duress to explain why he had not hung the picture, or what he had done with it. Worse than a gift of a picture is something like a mounted animal head (not likely to be given by a woman) or even a whole stuffed animal. William Manchester, in his early book on John Kennedy, reports how Vice-President Johnson pursued the President, relative to the whereabouts of a deer head he, the Vice-President, had had mounted for the President, until the latter, finally, put it on a wall in the White House.

The first intrusion of this kind probably occurred when a cave lady visited the cave of the first cave man who did the walldrawings in his cave, possibly in anticipation of the cave lady's visit. (Although it is generally assumed without good evidence that the early drawings were done by men, it is not necessarily so. The cave lady may have decorated her own cave.) In any case, the female visitor may very well have suggested to the cave man that he had done his drawings on the wrong wall, or that he had used a wrong color stone, or had not put the drawings in the best light, or that he had drawn them too high on the wall.

Next to a mounted head, giving some person a representation of his sign of the zodiac is most intrusive. He may not be into astrology, or may not like his sign, or the representation of it, a threefold risk. Whereas there is no sure defense against the picture-intrusion invasion, or possibly incursion, there are some evasive and delaying and diversionary techniques that are helpful. I have established themes for certain rooms. If the picture given me does not conform to the room theme, obviously and logically, or at least for the sake of consistency, it cannot be hung in the room. I now have three such rooms. My living room is reserved for Currier and Ives prints or paintings of horses and hounds. My study, the second protected area, is restricted to representations of authors or artists whom I accept. I am now holding the line with Walt Whitman, James Joyce, Cervantes, William Butler Yeats, Sean O'Casey, and Thomas More.

The third room, recently added to the protected list, is my dining room for which, under extreme pressures to hang a gift picture, I declared that the theme was birds, limited to fighting cocks and Audubon drawings and of more or less domestic, or near domestic, game birds like grouse and wild turkeys.

The other rooms of my house, a second study, a hallway and staircase, two bedrooms, a kitchen, and three bathrooms, are still areas of controversy and of compromise.

If the male homeowner has a dog even the dog's rights and privileges and properties may become the subject of abuse. The dog's toys may be found, after the visitor leaves, in a neat pile in a corner of a room or in a hall. A rawhide bone may have been washed, much to the dog's displeasure, the dog dish run through the dishwasher, and even the dog's blanket put into or through a washing machine. I have never seen or heard of these things having been done to a woman's dog or cat, or to their things, by anyone but the possessor of the pet, or with permission. Not so in the case of men's pets.

Carrol Jenkins

Remembering and Remembered

THE DEATH OF CARROL JENKINS of Rappahannock County early in the month of November of 1988 was little noted beyond the limits of the county. Within the county, however, especially in the western part, he is missed. Something, someone, a force of weight, is missing. There seems to be a slight wobble in the axis of the county. Things are not quite as they were. His voice and comments are missing in the country store. His familiar pickup truck not seen on the county roads. It was not that Carrol did anything of particular or great significance for the county, as a country doctor might have done, or a lawyer or a land owner, a clergyman, or a banker. He filled in; he did what needed to be done.

Carrol made his living principally by buying and selling, by trading and bartering—used cars, and especially used pickup trucks, and horses and cattle. The margins of gain in his transactions were usually slight, like those of a Wall Street broker operating in a tight market. He did not take advantage, but dealt largely with others who knew the trade.

His commercial deportment and relationships were almost purely professional. If he had been dealing in England rather than in Rappahannock County, he undoubtedly would have conducted his business in guineas, along with other professional classes, rather than in pounds and pence.

For nearly ten years he "looked after" my house and small piece of land in the county. No bill was ever presented, nor were fees mentioned, unless he had to hire extra help. I tried to anticipate what I owed him, or what I would owe him, usually leaving a check on the garden tractor seat. If I were in arrears he would casually mention what work he had done in recent days or weeks, or trips he had to take to nearby towns for supplies or repairs. So our relationship survived, even flourished. When he said "don't worry" when I was to be gone from my house for a week or more, I didn't worry.

I was never sure of his reading skills, but he spoke well. He knew animal signs and could read the weather and foretell its changes, not just by day or week, but by seasons. Heavy flowering of locust trees meant a good corn crop, for example.

Carrol was a large man, tall and heavy, somewhat too heavy, but his weight added to his dignity. He carried himself straight, upright, in part because of a back injury incurred, according to a local report, when as a younger man, demonstrating his strength (reputed to have been the greatest in the county), he had, in lifting the end of a tractor, injured a disc or two in his lower back. An additional reason for his upright bearing was that he was blind in one eye, the result of his having been hit in the one eye by a shotgun pellet, while driving birds to waiting hunters. The pellet hole still showed, like the pupil hole drilled in ancient statues.

The combination of the bad back and of the partial blindness gave great dignity and balance to his every move. He always held the center in careful balance, while all else revolved around him. He shifted his weight carefully.

What he did best, what will be missed the most, was to remember—the former residents of the county, the old days, the transitions. He had been there when in the '30s the National Park had been established in the Blue Ridge Mountains, when the mountain farms were taken over by the government, the mountain people displaced and moved out of the mountain. He was there in the '70s and '80s when farm consolidations began to occur, and real estate speculators and income-tax farmers bought up small holdings, turning them into cattle operations or simply holding them waiting for increase in land values in a kind of modern enclosure movement. He protested the tearing down of farm buildings, vacant cabins, and houses, and especially of the chimneys and fireplaces. The old places, he held, should be left as "reminders" of who had lived there, at least until there were no persons who cared to remember, or to be reminded.

Ruin of Hand's Grist Mill, Rt. 618

THE VIEW FROM RAPPAHANNOCK
II
By Eugene J. McCarthy

It was five years ago when Eugene J. McCarthy wrote his first book about Virginia's Rappahannock County, his country home 75 miles and 75 years away from Washington, D.C. He was green back then; the view was a newcomer's. But a few years of early morning discussions at the W. and J. store have seasoned him to local life, and he can say with some authority now that "nothing in the county is ever quite as simple as it seems."

Finding a "merkle" isn't simple. On occasion the former presidential candidate and senator from Minnesota has found these tasty mushrooms in the woods, but just as often he's resorted to begging for them. He's accepted anonymous gifts. Successful merkle hunting seems to involve blue eyes and the right kind of cap.

And one of these days McCarthy just might master his Lynch's Fool Proof Turkey Call (Model 101). He could virtually hold court at the country store if he managed it. So far he's drawing mostly crows.

These are only a couple of samples from this new edition of Rappahannock stories, tales, musings and reminiscences by perhaps the last American politician to carry an ounce of poetry in his blood. So lean back, get comfortable and read about a scientific study of roadside trash, fitting chickens with contact lenses and "that treacherous gland, your prostate;" about the personalities behind fence types, a proposal for uncle's day and women who assault the comforts of a single man's domain; and why this political man broke his own rule against going to the aid of a columnist in distress. It had something to do with a skunk.

EPM PUBLICATIONS
McLEAN, VIRGINIA

ISBN 0-939009-19-6

$12.95